MW01234298

"Steve Brown's book will surprise you. It is, ~~~~ ~~~~,
conveys. With a well researched approach, Brown develops the "Big Three" premises in the title; his conclusions will inspire and challenge you. It is obvious from the beginning that Steve Brown is an ardent follower of Jesus, and is seeking to live a genuinely Christ-centered life before God and people. I highly recommend this thought-provoking book. Whether you agree with his conclusions or not, you will be stirred."
Dr. J. Douglas Gehman, President, Globe International Pensacola, Florida

"The title is shocking and the contents amazing! This is truly a new display of grace directly from the word of God. Every Christian, historian, and even atheist should read this book, highly recommended!"
Wayne Sutton, TheSecondAdam.com

"After Reading over 300 Christian titles (including the Bible), there's no doubts this book will shift your thoughts, challenge your beliefs, and open your heart to the true grace and love of God. I bought it out of pure curiosity, studied it with eyes wide open, and fell even deeper in love with the truths that most people have never been taught before!"
Rome Batchelor, Entrepreneur

"In this book, the author, in keeping with the tradition of Ezra who read the entire scroll of the Torah to the people, and interpreted the deeper meanings of the stories of the Torah to the assembled crowd, is showing how the scripture can be made meaningful to today's time. In the old days, the words were spoken as a story and explained based on the needs of the moment. Later, fear of loss, created the written word which became dogma. I applaud the effort to resurrect the tradition of telling these beautiful stories and embellish them with a moral lesson germane to current affairs."
Sam Gill, Professor, San Francisco State University

"Of course, Jesus drank wine. Of course, Judas had some regrets. Of course, some Old Testament prophets used the metaphor that God was like a faithful husband to his people Israel, but Israel was so unfaithful to God that God must divorce her. If this were all, the book would be proving the obvious. But, time after time the book proved to be a powerful presentation and promotion of the most basic ideas of Christianity, loving, giving, and forgiving. And it manages to get this message across, not in the stuffy, pompous language of many sermons, but in delightfully colloquial English. Enjoy it!"

James T. McDonough, Jr., Ph.D. from Columbia University and Biblical Studies Professor at a number of Universities

"A fresh look that reawakens the well-known stories of the Bible and sends you digging to hear more. It keeps you engaged and alert and reminds you not to be a lazy learner."

Robin Willis, Southern female presbyterian running a local Bible study

SECOND EDITION

Jesus Drank, Judas Repented and God Divorced His Bride

By Steve Brown

20660 Stevens Creek Blvd., Suite 210
Cupertino, CA 95014

Published by Happy About®
20660 Stevens Creek Blvd., Suite 210, Cupertino, CA 95014
http://happyabout.com

First Printing: September 2007
Second Printing: June 2011
Paperback ISBN: 978-1-60005-201-9 (1-60005-201-0)
eBook ISBN: 978-1-60005-202-6 (1-60005-202-9)
Place of Publication: Silicon Valley, California, USA
Paperback Library of Congress Number: 2011930556

Subject: Religious-Christian, Spiritual: Faith-Based

Trademarks

Warning and Disclaimer

Why Read This Book?

This book seeks to stir up heightened interest in what the Bible says by questioning even the most primary, and most popular biblical teachings. Here are a few examples of common biblical knowledge challenges:

- Ask anybody how many animals of each kind Noah took on the ark and they'll probably say two. However, God told Noah to take fourteen of most. Yes, there were fourteen reindeer on the ark!

- The prophet Ezra blessed a divorce and proclaimed that the men should "be of good courage, and do it" (Ezra 10:3–5). God divorced Israel (Isaiah 50:1). Now please, make no mistake, this book isn't pro-divorce or pro-drunkenness. Rather, it was written to provide Bible based hope, no matter your current station in life and in spite of all of your failures, past, present, and future. God's grace has you covered!

- Regarding forgiveness, Mathew 27:3 clearly states that Judas
  a) repented,
  b) confessed his sin publicly, and
  c) gave the money back. So, with Christ standing in earshot of this confession, two questions arise regarding Judas: Would Christ forgive Judas? Did Christ forgive him?

Most religious books are largely "sugar coated" and noncontroversial. But, the Bible isn't that way. Neither is this book. In the Bible, you'll discover that God can be quite a dramatic God. Christ was not popular because he gave everybody "warm fuzzies," rather; he was strong in his understanding of the Hebrew law and also in his intolerance for arrogance and self-righteousness.

This book delivers to the reader:

- A far greater understanding of the Bible and its implications
- A deep biblical understanding of forgiveness, and our responsibility to forgive
- Examples of common biblical knowledge that is challenged

When it comes to real-life issues, many people are unsure and/or unaware of the simplistic guidance the Bible offers. Why? Perhaps the subjects are too controversial to talk about in a church setting. Using solid biblical references, this book seeks to stir up heightened interest in what the Bible says by questioning even the most primary and most popular biblical teachings.

Dedication

To those of us who are ADHD.

Acknowledgements

I wish to thank all those who helped me.

A special thanks to Nina Louviere for providing a place where I could live and work on this project during the past two years. Her generosity is excelled by none and can't be over-emphasized. Without her help, I could not have written this work.

James T. McDonough, Jr., Ph.D., whose editing and advice saved my literary life.

Mitchell Levy, CEO, Happy About, whose faith and patience made this possible. Thanks for taking a chance on a rookie like me.

Jon & Angela Sahim for their financial support, their faith in me to complete the task and their encouragement and excitement in the project.

Mom & Dad for taking me to church regularly (even when I didn't want to go).

A Message From Happy About®

Thank you for your purchase of this Happy About book. It is available online at http://happyabout.com/myfaith/jesusdrank.php or at other online and physical bookstores.

- Please contact us for quantity discounts at sales@happyabout.info
- If you want to be informed by e-mail of upcoming Happy About® books, please e-mail bookupdate@happyabout.info

Happy About is interested in you if you are an author who would like to submit a non-fiction book proposal or a corporation that would like to have a book written for you. Please contact us by e-mail editorial@happyabout.info or phone (1-408-257-3000).

Other Happy About books available include:

- Happy About My Christian Faith:
  http://happyabout.com/myfaith/mychristianfaith.php
- Moving From Vision to Reality:
  http://happyabout.com/myfaith/vision2reality.php
- 30-Day Bootcamp: Your Ultimate Life Makeover:
  http://happyabout.com/30daybootcamp/life-makeover.php
- Tales From the Networking Community:
  http://happyabout.com/networking-community.php
- Happy About Online Networking:
  http://happyabout.com/onlinenetworking.php
- I'm on LinkedIn—Now What???:
  http://happyabout.com/linkedinhelp.php
- Happy About Animals:
  http://happyabout.com/animals.php
- Foolosophy:
  http://happyabout.com/foolosophy.php
- Happy About Joint Venturing:
  http://happyabout.com/jointventuring.php

Contents

How I Fought for My Life without Losing My Soul

Since that fateful January night there have been no coincidences in my life. Each important event has lead to something good for me, my family, and because you are holding this book, you. The pages in this book outline how I fought for my life without losing my soul and why I know you can do the same.

I would've graduated from Pine Forest High School in Pensacola, Florida, in 1978, but they asked me to leave. During my eleventh grade school year the guidance counselor called my parents and said, "Steve can't learn. The best thing you can do for him is to take him out of school and place him in a vocational school so that he can learn a trade. Then perhaps someday he can become a self-supporting member of society." Understand that the term ADHD was not yet known.

I've been a husband. I married at age—nineteen. I've been through a hard divorce. I am a father and a single parent. I have teenagers. I've been homeless and penniless. I've been a millionaire twice, and lost it all twice. With the exception of one eight-month span, I've been self-employed my entire adult life. My hobby: collecting signed memorabilia.

In the past twenty-five years I've built two businesses from my garage. One became a national food manufacturing company, cooking a half-million food products per day. When I sold it in 1996, our products were the trendsetter in the industry. The other is an international shipping company of which I own today.

I'm sharing this with you because I want you to know that I've been where many of you currently are, or will be at some point in the future. I know what it feels like to live in your car. To have your phone turned off. I've been in the parking lot of Wal-Mart, having had to choose between food and gas. I know what it feels like when your closest family members say and do hurtful things to you. I know how it feels to be physically abused, alone, scared, and with no one to turn to.

I also know what happened the day I accepted Christ as my savior. Everything changed. That day, "stuff" started happening. Good stuff. And the more I sought him, the better it got. Don't get me wrong: I've worked more one hundred-plus hour weeks than I ever want to remember. But I've lived a blessed, "magical" life. Moreover, my kids are all good citizens and I am very proud of their work and station in life. And through it all, my children will tell you that they feel we have one of the most stable families they know of.

I'm also both corporately and personally debt free. Almost each day of the week I can choose whether to work or travel, write or fish. I am blessed in spite of myself! You can be too! I've made a lot of mistakes since that January night. But they don't define who I am. And yours don't define who you are. Just keep asking for mercy and grace. He'll keep giving!

Introduction

Dinner is fabulous at the Australian-style steak house. However, we've opted to go for dessert a few blocks away. Leaving the restaurant, we move through the doorway and onto the front walk where our attention is immediately drawn down the street to the sound of somebody shouting.

Across the parking lot, I can see him pacing along the side of the busy city street. His calls to "repent," aimed at patrons entering another restaurant, echo through the entire restaurant area. He is a street preacher.

The management of the family-friendly, world-famous, Irish restaurant on Gregory Street in Pensacola has posted a member of their bagpipe band outside, close to the front door. Under French-style streetlights, the sounds from the seasoned Irishman's instrument drowns out the preacher's shouts.

Night is falling and stars dot the cool, spring evening sky. Well-groomed, landscaped hedges and park benches along the tree-lined sidewalk adorn the front side of the Irish restaurant. The restaurant is busy, and the park benches are filled with patrons, talking as they wait to be seated. A man, holding a sleeping child in his arms, peers through the shrubs and across the street, watching the preacher pace angrily along the street.

Perhaps the screamer feels this is his calling in life. Whatever his reason, he needs to do a little more homework. I'm no scholar, but as I listen to his rant it seems obvious he has little knowledge of what he's yelling about. I'm thinking, "Somebody needs to do something. He's an embarrassment to the cause of Christ."

He's screaming, "Repent! You're going to hell!" Yet, how would he know whether or not the people standing in line are going to hell? He knows nothing about any of them. It looks to me as if they're going to dinner. And it's safe to guess that some will probably be in church on Sunday.

It's a Tuesday night dinner crowd, for goodness sake. If he's absolutely set on preaching a little "hell fire and brimstone," there's an adult nightclub a half block down the street. Perhaps their steady flow of clients would be more deserving of his preaching.

I head straight for him but my friend, Nina, will have nothing to do with it. She opts to slide into the front seat of the truck as I start walking across the parking lot. As I reach the sidewalk I wait for him to pace back to where I'm standing.

Clad in a brown plaid shirt and straw hat, the preacher chews nervously on a matchstick stuck in the corner of his mouth. His skin-tight, navy blue jeans strike him well above his ankles and he is wearing suspenders. The large black Bible rolled up in his right hand doubles as his bullhorn. A dozen homemade signs stuck on the ground serve as his backdrop as he shouts at the scores of waiting patrons. He glances at me as he paces toward me, and his shouting continues without interruption.

Have you ever noticed that there's a lot of confidence that goes along with ignorance? The moment I say hello, he confirms that my five-second assessment of him as a moron is justified. "Look," he growls angrily, "unless you've got something important, I don't have time to talk to you. If you just want to chat or you've got some questions, go over and talk to my wife and she can help you."

I resist from bursting out into laughter. Does this guy, who looks like the poster child for a hillbilly anger management class, actually think anybody would look to him for any kind of help? Glancing past him, I can see his wife standing a few steps up the sidewalk. She's holding a homemade sign that reads, "REPENT OR BURN."

I ask, "Do you know how many animals of each kind Noah took on the Ark?" Instantly, his eyes seem to glaze over and he has that "deer-in-the-headlights" look. With forehead wrinkled, eyes squinted, nostrils flared, and cheeks puffed out like a blowfish, he snarls, "How many animals of each kind Noah took on that Ark doesn't mean anything to anybody, son. Why in the world would anybody care about that? Noah and them there animals ain't got nothin' to do with anything important!"

I reply calmly, "You don't know the answer, do you?" There is a moment of silence as I look at him in the eyes and tell him, "Noah took fourteen each of most all the animals.[1] But, you don't know your Bible very well, do you?" He huffs and puffs and then he does something quite odd. He puts his hands over his ears, spins around on his heels and takes off running down the sidewalk to where his wife is standing, all the while screaming like his hair is on fire.

When he stops, he quickly turns back toward those at the restaurant and resumes shouting. Gradually, he meanders back down to where I'm standing. I open the conversation again, "Did you know that Jesus drank, Judas repented and God divorced his bride?" He jumps back and gasps for breath. Again, he grabs his ears and takes off running and screaming.

Up the sidewalk, he stops, spins around and faces me. He leans forward with his hands on his knees, as though he just finished running a marathon. After a few moments, he leans backward, staring into the sky before straightening his back. He begins moving toward me. However, this time he's not shouting at the people across the street. With his hands stuck into his front pockets, he walks along slowly, staring at the ground as though he's in deep thought, until he's one small step in front of me.

---

1. Genesis 7:2

As he leaned forward toward me, his deep whisper is alarming, "You must be one of those boys who thinks that Christ's message was all about love, huh? You're one of those, aren't you? Well you're wrong, pal!"

The thought of trying to reason with him crosses my mind, but I know that I'm wasting my time. He didn't come up to me seeking an intelligent conversation.

Calmly, I offer my closing words, "You're an angry man. And in the name of Christ, you stand here on the roadside spewing out hostility and judgment on people you don't know. Neither do you know your Bible. Christ summed up his entire message with these words, 'Love God and love your neighbor.'[2] Christ reserved most of his harsh words for the 'religious crowd.' In fact, he was a friend to sinners." Once again, the preacher places his hands over his ears, turns around, and runs up the street.

Then, as he had done before, he rolls his Bible into the shape of a bullhorn and raises it to his mouth. However, he doesn't turn toward the patrons across the street; instead, he turns toward me and begins screaming, "You're a sinner! You're on your way to hell..., blah, blah, blah, blah, blah."

I wait for him to come closer; however, he stays up the street. I glance over at the truck where Nina is patiently waiting. She gives me that "look." I oblige her, and we leave and go for ice cream.

Christ said, "Love God and love your neighbor as yourself." Being saved by "faith in Christ" means confessing your sins and surrendering to God. The Apostle Paul explained that the Law of Moses is over and done with, replaced by love.[3] Instead of having a checklist of things to do, and avoid as if we are earning gold stars, we're to concentrate on loving God and people. The point is, if we love people, we won't murder them, steal from them, threaten them, condemn them, judge them, and so on.

---

2. Matthew 22:35
3. Romans 10:4

Coming to the knowledge that Noah took fourteen reindeer on the ark[4] is not necessarily a life-changing revelation. However, the fact that every storybook in Christian bookstores says it's two should raise a concern. I mean, in every book, the story is told wrong. Don't believe it? Go check it out. Apparently a lot of authors forgot to read a Bible before they wrote their stories.

In the first chapter of this book, you'll find a children's short story— "David and the Princess: The Untold Story of David and Goliath." Again, not a life-changing revelation. However, this story will demonstrate that the real story of David and Goliath is not what most of us have been taught: It's not a story about a small, twelve-year-old boy with miraculous slinging skills who kills a giant! No, it's a story far more believable than that.

The true story is about fear, courage, and the pursuit of a dream. It's about obeying your parents, responsibility, and developing your talents. Unfortunately, this story has hardly, if ever, been taught.

You'll probably be surprised. You may even be skeptical but when you've finished reading, decide which version would benefit children the most. Will it be "David and the Princess," or the questionable, watered down version that's been taught for decades? If you have young children or grandchildren, I encourage you to read "David and the Princess" to them as they will probably enjoy it.

How many of you were taught that God divorced his bride? How many church sign boards have you seen that read, "Next Sunday's Sermon: Jesus Drank!" or "Judas Repented!" It's probably safe to say, "None." *Jesus Drank, Judas Repented and God Divorced His Bride* lays many topics on the table that are rarely ever discussed. When you have finished reading, and have conducted your own research, you may be surprised by your discoveries.

Why bother to write such a controversial piece of literature? It's simple: To send you scrambling for your Bible to see if what you are reading is true. Tighten your seatbelts! This book is a roller-coaster ride through Bible facts, current world events, and historical evidence that can no longer be avoided.

---

4. Genesis 7:2

1 David and the Princess

True or False

Let's begin by taking a quick "True or False" quiz: As you read the ten statements below, decide which are true and which aren't. If you don't want to mark on the page, use a separate piece of paper, and write either "T" or "F" so you'll be able to count the number of T's and F's when finished.

Let's get started!

True or False

1.	John F. Kennedy was a ventriloquist	T or F
2.	Fats Domino never had a number one hit	T or F
3.	A bank in Utah was built from bricks sent through the mail	T or F
4.	The Internet was invented by the government and was first called the "Galactic Network"	T or F
5.	God divorced his bride	T or F
6.	Tomatoes are a fruit	T or F
7.	According to the Bible, you can commit suicide and go to paradise	T or F
8.	Photic sneeze reflex is a medical condition by which people exposed to bright light involuntarily sneeze	T or F
9.	The Mad Hatter in Alice in Wonderland was a symbolic character for hat makers during the late 1800s who were exposed to mercury, causing psychosis and requiring them to be declared "mad"	T or F
10.	Tim Allen's real name is Tim Dick	T or F

If a true or false quiz seems like an unusual way to start, well, it is. Take a moment to total up the number of answers you marked true and the number you marked false. Now check out the answers below.

Answers

1. True. John F. Kennedy was an accomplished ventriloquist.
2. True. Fats Domino never had a number one hit.
3. True. "When W. H. Coltharp, in charge of building the Bank of Vernal, Utah, was confronted with the task of getting bricks for the bank, he turned to the Parcel Post Service. Instead of paying four times the cost of the bricks for them to be shipped by wagon freight, Coltharp arranged for the bricks to be shipped in 50-pound packages, through the Parcel Post Service, a ton at a time." Source: National Postal Museum.

4. True. The Internet was invented by the government and was first called the "Galactic Network." The Internet was initially developed in 1973 by American computer scientist Vinton Cerf as part of a project sponsored by the United States Department of Defense Advanced Research Projects Agency (DARPA). The Internet began as a computer network that linked computer networks at several universities and research laboratories in the United States. In 1989, English computer scientist Timothy Berners-Lee developed the World Wide Web for the European Organization for Nuclear Research.

5. True. In Isaiah 50:1 and Jeremiah 3:8, God proclaims his divorce decree to Israel.

6. True. The tomato is a fruit.

7. True. King Saul committed suicide. During a séance held by a witch the day before, God's prophet Samuel, who was in paradise, told Saul,"... Tomorrow you and your sons will be with me."[5]

8. True. The photic sneeze reflex is a medical condition by which people exposed to bright light involuntarily sneeze.

9. True. The making of felt hats of the day required use of large amounts of mercury. In the late 1800s it was determined that extended exposure to mercury causes brain damage, or psychosis, which led to the term "mad as a hatter."

10. True. Tim Allen's real name is Tim Dick.

Like many, you may have thought that some of the statements were false; that's okay. And if you liked some of this trivia, you'll probably enjoy the rest of this book.

The story of David and the Princess demonstrates how the famous Bible story of David and Goliath could have been written a long time ago. Let's review some of the facts that are often overlooked in most accounts of the story:

---

5. I Samuel 28:19 and 31:4 NIV

- David was about seventeen or eighteen years old.

- David was already considered a "mighty valiant man, and a man of war" by King Saul's court before the confrontation with Goliath.

- Experts agree that during the time before the story 700 of David's closest friends were Benjamite soldiers who were experts with a sling. It was the only weapon they carried into battle.

- At first, David ran in fear from Goliath, along with everybody else. In the next verse he is in the army camp, where he inquired, and was told three times that the man who killed the giant would be rewarded with the princess's hand in marriage, a wealth of riches, and the promise that he and his family would never have to pay taxes again.

In case you're shaking your head and asking yourself whether or not this is true, relax. At the end of this story, you'll find scripture references to validate all of the statements above plus a few extra points you may notice within this story.

Throughout his lifetime, David demonstrated that he was fallible, just like you and me, and that he had a strong faith in God. Neither of these hindered him from pursuing his dreams or God's purpose in his life. David was a man of strong faith. He was also a talented, valiant warrior.

On this particular day, it is evident that David's core motivation for putting his life at risk was not solely for the cause of righteousness. Remember, he proved his human side when he, along with all of the other soldiers, ran in fear from the giant.

It wasn't until later in the day that David learned about the life-changing reward from the king awaiting the man who kills Goliath. It's then that he begins to voice his defense of the army of God. It was then that he inquired three times about the reward, and from two different sources. After verifying the details, he negotiates with the king for the opportunity to fight to his death for God and his country against a professional, championed opponent.

During the fight, David demonstrates why he had already been referred to as a "mighty valiant man, and a man of war." Unbeknown to most, David could sling a stone with almost as much accuracy and velocity as a modern day rifle shoots a bullet. While all of the other soldiers may have looked at Goliath and thought, "He's too big to hit!" David must have thought, "He's too big to miss."

David and the Princess

The Untold Story of David and Goliath

In the small village of Bethlehem, in a house by a river, David lived with his father, mother, and seven brothers. David was seventeen years old and quite handsome with his flowing hair and beautiful eyes.

At the foot of the tree-covered mountain, white sheep grazed in the green hillsides of the ranch. David and the other ranch hands protected his father's herds day and night and kept them fed and watered.

Around their waists, the ranch hands wore small leather pouches filled with small stones and a leather sling. They used these to fight off wild animals that came to steal their sheep. David was an expert with his sling, as were many of his friends.

One evening at sunset, a lion slipped down the side of the mountain and began chasing the sheep. David jumped up from the campfire and ran toward the lion, reaching into his pouch and loading a stone into the sling. When the lion saw David it stopped chasing the sheep and stood motionless, staring at David. Then the lion began trotting toward him, roaring and taunting. David stopped running, and took aim at the lion, which was now coming quite fast, David fired his sling.

The stone buzzed loudly as it flew fast across the field. A loud "pop" echoed through the valley as the stone struck the lion between its eyes and sank deep into its forehead. The lion stumbled, fell to the ground, and died.

"Great shot, David!" Matthew exclaimed as he ran out onto the edge of the pasture. Matthew was David's best friend and was helping David watch over the sheep when the lion came. David and Matthew laughed and talked as they walked toward the wagon, climbed onboard, and rode across the field to where the lion lay breathless.

"That was a close one, David. You had me worried," Matthew exclaimed as they loaded the lion onto the horse-drawn wagon. The two boys jumped onboard and David rode the wagon to the barn.

David's father was in the barn sharpening an ax when the boys arrived. "That's a frightful looking beast," he said, as he gazed at the large, dead lion. "Thank God you weren't hurt," he said in a concerned tone. As he was speaking, the sound of the dinner bell rang across the meadow. It was time for dinner.

David's father spoke as they moved along. "I have an errand for you, David. Tomorrow, I want you to take some cheese and bread to your brothers." Some of David's brothers were in the army and David often took supplies to them. "I'll leave at daylight, Father," David said. David loved the adventure of the battle and was anxious for the day when he could join the king's army.

At daylight, David's mother was cooking breakfast for David, Matthew, and all the other ranch hands. The smell of fresh-baked bread filled the early morning air. At the breakfast table, David reminded the other hands, "Keep a sharp eye on the sheep while I'm gone today." Then, as he took another biscuit from the pile, David exclaimed to Matthew in an excited tone, "Let's go see my brothers!" And with that, the two young men headed out of the door and to the barn.

In the barn, David's father had just finished hitching the horses to the wagon. "Make sure you ask and see that your brothers are well," his father remarked gently. "I will, Father," David said. He climbed on the wagon and with one loud "Pop!" of the reins, the horses trotted out of the barn.

As they approached the camp, David looked down the side of the mountain and noticed that all the soldiers were lined up for battle. Some were on horses and some were on foot. "Wait here with the wagon," David told Matthew. He jumped down to the ground and began running down the side of the mountain.

As he ran, David could see the archenemies of Israel, the Philistines, on the far side of the canyon. It looked as though both armies were preparing for battle. At the foot of the mountain, David found his brothers. They were on the front row of the battle line.

No sooner than David arrived, a deep, thundering voice echoed across the valley. David turned to look. Standing on the other side of the mountain stream was a giant over nine feet tall. His name was Goliath. He began pacing back and forth, taunting and cursing the king's army. "Send me a man!" Goliath yelled. "Send out a man! He and I will fight! If he beats me, then we will be your servants. But if I win the fight, then you will be our servants!"

Every soldier in the king's army was speechless and frozen in fear. After a few moments of silence, David and all the rest of the men in the army turned back and ran. They were so afraid that they ran back up the side of the mountain and into the safety of the army camp.

Warming his hands by the fire, David overheard two soldiers as they talked, "Did you hear what the reward is for the man who kills Goliath?" The other soldier quickly replied, "Yes, he gets to marry the princess! And the king is going to make him rich in gold, and he will never have to pay taxes again."

David spoke up quickly, "What did you say was the reward for the man who kills the giant?" The soldiers turned toward David and one of them answered, "The man who kills the giant gets to marry the princess, and the king will make him rich in gold, and he will never have to pay taxes again."

David was unaware that his oldest brother was standing nearby listening to the conversation. "What are you doing here?" he said in a jealous, angry tone. "You can't help with this problem. You need to go home and get back to watching those sheep. Who's doing that for you?"

David looked at his brother and said, "What have I done to cause you to be angry with me? Aren't the rewards from the king and the insults to God enough reason for me to act?" David continued in a confident tone, "This giant has embarrassed and challenged the armies of the living God. And you, Brother, should have already done something about this."

Turning away, David walked across the camp to another soldier and asked, "What is the reward for the man who kills the giant?" The eyes of the soldier gleamed, "The man who kills the giant gets to marry the princess, and the king is going to make him rich in gold, and neither he nor his family will ever have to pay taxes again."

"I'll do this," David proclaimed in a serious and confident tone. "I'll go down and fight him. He can't stand against me. I've fought with a bear and a lion and killed them both. The Lord helped me to stand against them and with God's help, I'll beat this guy. He's challenging the armies of the living God and the Lord will deliver him into my hands today."

The king's senior lieutenant was standing close by and overheard David. Hoping to encourage David, the captain said, "If you want to fight the giant, you must first ask the king." David turned to him and said, "I'll speak with the king. Take me to him." With a slight smile spreading on his face, the captain asked, "You do know that to join the king's army you must be twenty years old?" David answered confidently, "I may only be eighteen, but just get me an audience with the king. He will decide whether I can go and fight."

"Before you can speak with the king, you must first tell me what you plan to say," the captain demanded. David shared his stories about the bear and the lion. The captain moved on as they spoke, "I'm not sure that the king will allow you to fight the giant. The entire future of the nation may be decided in this single battle, but I will take you to him, and you can make your request."

They walked on, passing several rows of tan-colored tents before stopping in front of one. Two soldiers guarded the entrance. "Open," the captain commanded and the guards pulled the tent flaps back. David and the captain stepped inside.

Inside, the air was warm and stuffy and torches dimly lit the area. The king and his men were standing in a circle, speaking softly among themselves. The king acknowledged the captain and David as they walked inside. Stepping forward, the captain spoke. "Dear king, please allow me to introduce your brave and loyal subject, David. He wishes to fight with the giant."

The king tilted his head slightly as he stared at David and answered with a surprised tone, "Is that so?" David replied "There's no further reason to be afraid of the giant. I'll fight him."

The king spoke as he pondered over David's words, "Your idea may be noble, David, however, you don't appear to be a trained soldier. I'm confident you won't be able to stand against this man and you will certainly be killed if you go up against him. Goliath is a professional soldier, trained to kill since he was a small boy. You cannot prevail over him."

"You're right," David said calmly. "I'm not a skilled soldier. However, I am a valiant opponent. Moreover, God has appointed Goliath to die today and God has prepared me to do it. I am sure of this."

"Not long ago, a bear came and took a lamb out of my father's flock. I shot a stone from my sling and knocked him down. As I went to rescue the lamb, the bear awoke and attacked me. I grabbed him by his beard and beat him to death with my club. Yesterday, I killed a lion with a single stone from my sling. I've defended my flock from bears and lions many times with my own hands. Goliath is going to die just as they did. He has come against the army of the living God and the Lord will deliver him into my hands. He will not prevail."

The eyes of the king were fixed on David's face. Stroking his beard, he pondered David's words. Every eye in the tent was fixed on the king. After a few moments, the king nodded his head in approval. "All right...you may go and fight with him. May God bless you and give you a victory today. However," the king continued, "since you don't have any armor of your own, I want you to use mine." David agreed, and the king's men began strapping the king's armor onto David's arms, legs, and chest.

With the armor secretly in place, David paced inside the tent and tried to spin his sling. David had never practiced slinging stones while wearing armor and it got in the way of his swing.

"I will not be able to wear these," David said. "I've not trained wearing armor and I cannot wear it today. All I need is my sling and my club." Rubbing his beard, the king nodded his head in agreement and the soldiers began removing the armor.

As he stepped out from the tent, the cool desert breeze blew softly across David's face. The king and his men followed him out of the tent and watched as he walked over to the rushing mountain stream. Nobody spoke. The only sound was that of the waterfall in the mountain rocks above.

David knelt beside the clear, icy-cold stream where he carefully looked through the stones, knowing that only smooth, round stones fly straight. It was rumored that Goliath had four brothers. To prepare, David took five stones from the stream and dropped them into his pouch as he stood. Then, nodding confidently at the curious group of soldiers who were watching, he walked toward the edge of the cliff, where he jumped off the ledge and began running down the mountainside.

The giant noticed that someone was running down the mountain toward him. "Finally, King Saul has come to fight with me!" Goliath thought to himself amusingly. He could hardly wait!

When Goliath saw young David, he yelled, "What do you think you're doing? Surely King Saul didn't send *you* out to fight with me!" Goliath was quite agitated to see that Saul, or one of his soldiers had not come to fight. "Where is your sword? Where is your shield and spear? Do you think you can come out here and beat me with a club as if I'm a dog?"

Meanwhile, David, who was running straight at the giant, was loading his sling with a stone. The giant, contemplating what appeared to be an unarmed opponent, now seemed somewhat amused by David. "If you keep running toward me, I'll feed your carcass to the vultures and the lions," the giant growled.

David proclaimed in a confident shout that echoed across the valley, "You're coming against me with a sword, a spear and a shield, but I'm coming against you in the name of the Lord of hosts, the God of the armies of Israel, whom you have boldly cursed and defied! You are the one who is appointed to die today and I'm going to cut your head off and feed your carcass to the vultures! All of the people in the land will know that the Lord does not need a sword and a spear to prevail! The battle is the Lord's, and he will deliver you into my hands today! All of the people throughout the nation will know that there is a God in Israel!" The giant had heard enough and began walking toward David.

As David ran toward the giant, the spinning sling made a curiously loud, humming sound. All eyes from both armies were fixed on David and the giant. The future of both nations was at stake. The winner would be decided by the outcome of the event unfolding in front of them.

Before the giant realized what David was doing, David had already slung the stone.

The stone flew fast across the valley and a loud, popping sound echoed through the canyon as it struck the brass helmet right between the eyes of the giant. The helmet shattered and the deadly stone sank deep into the giant's skull.

With his eyes closed, Goliath dropped slowly to his knees. After a few moments there came a loud "thud" as the giant kneeled forward and fell flat on his face. Silence fell across both mountainsides. All eyes were fixed on the lifeless Goliath and the young warrior.

David ran quickly towards him, grabbed Goliath's sword, and jumped up on the giant's back. Watching from a cliff, high above the battle, King Saul held his breath, as did most all of the other soldiers. David lifted the enormous sword high into the air and, in one swoop, sent Goliath's large, hairy head rolling down the hill into the rushing mountain stream below.

The deadly silence was broken and the valley erupted in yells and battle cries! Realizing that their champion was dead, the Philistine army began to run away. The soldiers in the king's army shouted with excitement as they chased after them.

David stayed at the scene of the battle. He walked down the mountainside trail and waded into the icy-cold water where he leaned over, reached in, and grabbed the giant's head. Holding it by the hair on top, he carried it up the side of the mountain and presented it to the king. The king declared in a somber tone, "That was an incredible victory...I have never seen anything like it."

David returned to where Goliath's body was lying, removed the giant's armor, and kept it for himself as a trophy. However, he took Goliath's sword, presented it to the priest, and requested that it be dedicated to God so that everybody in the land would always remember the day God delivered Israel from the hands of their enemy.

Soon, David and the king's youngest daughter, Princess Michal, were married. The story of David spread across the nation and its people loved him greatly.

Scripture References and Notes

David was a "mighty valiant man, and a man of war"	I Samuel 16:18
David and all the army ran in fear	I Samuel 17:24
The reward of the Princess	I Samuel 17:25, 26, 27, & 30
Goliath had four brothers	II Samuel 21:15–22
David takes Goliath's armor	I Samuel 17:54
The stone shattered Goliath's helmet	I Samuel 17:49, 50 of the Septuagint
Twenty-year age minimum for enlistment	Numbers 1:3

Experts agree that David most likely was an expert with a sling like many hundreds of other men in Israel at that time (Judges 20:16).

David's friends were experts at using a sling (I Chronicles 12:1, 2; Judges 20:16).

David was about seventeen or eighteen years old—The Bible doesn't give us an exact age for David when he fought Goliath; however we know from II Samuel 5:4 that "David was thirty years old when he began to reign, and he reigned forty years." So he was thirty when he ascended the throne. It was about fourteen years before this that he was anointed by Samuel and shortly after this that he fought Goliath. Therefore, David was between sixteen and twenty years of age when he fought and killed Goliath.

Practically Speaking

You've probably never heard the story of David and Goliath presented above. Clearly, David's attention was drawn to the rewards, which significantly motivated him to do what he did. And let's get real: Most people would jump at the opportunity to use their God-given talent to become an instant millionaire, marry the king's daughter, and become a national hero for the cause of God. Wouldn't you?

As we begin to review more important and yet controversial subjects in scripture, remember this: You should *not* be eager to accept what others (authors [like myself], pastors, teachers, etc.) tell you about the Bible. Rather, be a nobler person, like the people of Berea who "... received the message with great eagerness and examined the scriptures every day to see if what Paul said was true."[6]

Seatbelt fastened?

---

6. Acts 17:11 NIV

2 Jesus Drank

"Then exchange your tithe for silver...Use the silver to buy whatever you like: cattle, sheep, wine or other fermented drink, or anything you wish. Then you and your household shall eat there in the presence of the LORD your God and rejoice."

Deuteronomy 14:25, 26 NIV

Hospitality in Palestine

Wine has been made in Israel for about 6,000 years. However, many wines exported from Palestine were so bad that they had to be seasoned with honey, spices, and berries. Most resembled alcoholic versions of apricot pancake syrup rather than wine!

It is little wonder that when Christ turned water into wine, the director of the wedding said to the bridegroom, "Everyone brings out the choice wine first and then the cheaper wine after the guests have had too much to drink; but you have saved the best till now."[7] Could it have been a fine California Cabernet Sauvignon? Surely the

---

7. John 2:10 NIV

wine that Christ did create at the wedding feast was of high quality, or the director would not have spoken as he did. And history proves the fact that there was knowledge of high-quality wines in antiquity. Isaiah describes how the Lord will prepare a feast of well-aged, fine wines as a blessing.[8]

The book of Psalms credits God as the creator of "wine that gladdens the heart of man."[9] Proverbs explains that the reward and blessing for honoring the Lord with your wealth is prosperity and that your winepresses will be bursting with new wine.[10] The scriptures in Ecclesiastes says, "So go ahead. Eat your food and drink your wine with a happy heart, for God approves of this!"[11] It is also recommended that wine be given to the troubled to help them forget their problems.[12] Wine was used to make merry, and in worship and celebration before the Lord.[13]

After he began His ministry, Christ had no home and regularly depended on friends and acquaintances for shelter. He was a constant guest at dinners and banquets. Interestingly, we are given a glimpse into the eating and drinking habits of Christ when he compared himself with John the Baptist while addressing the stubbornness and hard-heartedness of the religious crowd, "... John the Baptist didn't drink wine and he often fasted, and you say, 'He's demon possessed.' And I, the Son of Man, feast and drink, and you say, 'He's a glutton and a drunkard, and a friend of the worst sort of sinners!'"[14] Even though Christ referred to himself as one who drinks wine, we know that he was never drunk.

Christ's need for hospitality took him into some unsavory places (by some standards). He established a reputation as a regular and welcomed houseguests of tax collectors and other "notorious sinners." Apparently, he was like that "special someone" whom you loved to see arriving and dreaded to see leaving. Imagine that!

---

8. Isaiah 25:6
9. Psalms 104:15 NIV
10. Proverbs 3:9–10
11. Ecclesiastes 9:7 NLT
12. Proverbs 31:6,7
13. II Samuel 13:28
14. Matthew 11:18, 19 NLT

Chapter 2: Jesus Drank

Was It Wine or Was It Grape Juice?

The same wine that made Noah, Lot, Nabal, Ahasuerus, and others drunk was given to Abraham by Melchizedek. The wine was kept in the storehouses of the kings of Israel and permitted to be given to all God's people.[15] Consider a few basic facts:

- Making wine requires three elements: water, sugar, and yeast. Grapes naturally contain all three.

- Wine is made from fermented grape juice. In Palestine, the moment a grape is crushed, it begins to ferment. Within three days, the alcohol content approaches an excess of 12%.

- The process required to pause fermentation is pasteurization. According to the United States Department of Agriculture, pasteurization was not invented until 1864.

- Except for drying grapes in the sun to make raisins, during the time of Christ there were no methods available to prevent fermentation of grape juice or to preserve whole grapes (for example, by freezing). There are no Greek or Hebrew words for nonalcoholic "grape juice."

- A careful examination of all the Hebrew words (as well as their cognates in other Semitic languages) and the Greek words for wine demonstrate that the ancients knew little about unfermented wine and made no attempts to preserve grape juice in an unfermented state.

- Wine and vinegar are both described as products containing alcohol.

- Noah was among the first to produce wine and is the first person in recorded history to become drunk.[16]

---

15. Genesis 9:21, 14:18, 19:32–35; I Samuel 25:37; Esther 1:7, 10; Isaiah 28:1, 7; Jeremiah 23:9; I Chronicles 27:27; II Chronicles 11:11; Nehemiah 5:18; Deuteronomy 14:26

16. Genesis 9:21

- The Hebrew word for "banquet" or "feast" literally means "drinking," which reveals much of the character of such occasions. The Greek word *sumposion* (symposium in English) means "drinking together." A certain amount of merriment was considered proper at a festival or a banquet.[17]

- Wine was the universal drink in antiquity. The temperate use of wine appears to have been a normal and accepted part of life.[18]

- The term "new" wine in Acts 2:13–15 was used to describe wine associated with public drunkenness, and not nonalcoholic grape juice. The word "new" was not in the Majority Text Greek manuscript of the book of Acts. The Greek manuscript of Acts reads, "... but others mocking were saying, 'They are filled of sweet wine.'" Between 1604 and 1611, King James I of England hired about fifty scholars and wrote his version of the Bible (the King James Bible, or KJV). It was during the writing of the KJV translation that the word "new" was placed within verse 13 of the second chapter of Acts.

- Christ said, "And no one after drinking old wine wants the new, for he says, 'The old is better.'"[19]

- The Law of Moses[20] dictated that wine mixed with water be used during Passover. Evidence strongly suggests that the wine used at the Lord's Supper was a mixture of water and wine, probably in a proportion of three to one, in agreement with the dictates of the Mishnah.

- Wine is mentioned about 230 times in the Bible, depending on which translation you are reading. Most of the time, it is mentioned with a positive or neutral connotation.

- Wine was an article of commerce.[21]

---

17. Genesis 43:34; Luke 5:34
18. Genesis 14:18; Judges 19:19; II Samuel 16:20
19. Luke 5:39 NIV
20. Leviticus 23:13
21. Ezekiel 27:18

The wine mentioned in the Bible was just that: wine. Wine contains varying amounts of alcohol. Within the Old and New Testaments, grape juice arguably appears to be referred to once[22] and the term "vinegar" is used several times. The Tyndale Bible Dictionary[23] defines wine as a "beverage made from fermented grape juice."

More positive (than negative) references to wine and strong drink appear in the scriptures. The same Hebrew and Greek words used to describe abuses are also used to speak of blessings. Furthermore, the Old Testament makes one distinction between wine and fresh grapes[24] and implies that when the word "wine" is used, the fermented drink is what the writer means.

In the Old Testament, "*Yayin*" is the usual Hebrew word for naturally fermented grape juice. It is usually referred to as "wine."[25]

In the New Testament, "*oinos*" is the usual word for "wine." Wine was a fermented beverage mixed with various amounts of water, and at times mixed with gall and myrrh.[26] The mention of the bursting of the wineskins[27] implies fermentation.

The New Testament argues clearly against the unrestrained use of wine. The biblical admonition is not to be drunk with wine.[28] Leaders in the Church were to practice moderation in the use of wine[29] and were not to be addicted to it.

God and the French Paradox

Perhaps God knows more about a healthy diet than we've given him credit. Almost without exception, when God mentions grape harvest a blessing, he also goes on to say that he will bless the crops of grain and olives. For example, "If you carefully obey all the commands I am

---

22. Numbers 6:3
23. Page 1302
24. Numbers 6:3
25. Genesis 14:18; 27:25
26. Matthew 27:34; Mark 15:23
27. Matthew 9:17; Mark 2:22; Luke 5:37
28. Ephesians 5:18; 1 Peter 4:3
29. I Timothy 3:3, 8; Titus 1:7

giving you today, and if you love the Lord your God with all your heart and soul, and if you worship him, then he will send the rains in their proper seasons so you can harvest crops of grain, grapes for wine, and olives for oil."[30]

The "French Paradox" is a name for the seemingly contradictory, yet true statement that people in France have a relatively low incidence of coronary heart disease, despite a diet allegedly rich in saturated fats. Clinical studies suggest that France's high consumption of red wine is the primary factor responsible for this. Many people in the Mediterranean community feel that those who don't drink red wine are actually harming their bodies. Paul, who wrote half of the books of the New Testament, prescribed wine to improve one's health.[31]

The traditional dietary patterns of the French population also include a high consumption of fruit, vegetables, bread, olive oil, and fish. Epidemiologists believe that low incidence of heart disease among the French may also be linked to eating less food per meal.[32] When God mentions grape harvest a blessing, he also goes on to say that he will bless the crops of grain and olives. This too is significant since gluttony is condemned in the Bible.

Biblical or Cultural Taboos?

Vinegar in Scripture

The word "vinegar" comes through French from the Latin *vinum*, meaning "wine," and the Latin *acer*, meaning "keen, sharp." *Oxos* in Greek can refer to poor-quality wine or to vinegar made from it. Vinegar was often called *oinos oxus* ("sharp wine") and was the ordinary drink of laborers and common soldiers.

Some say that Christ was offered vinegar during crucifixion. That is correct. In Palestine, cheap sour wine was referred to as vinegar, and the vinegar of that era contained varying amounts of alcohol. A range of four percent to fifteen percent alcohol by volume was common. Vinegar on the store shelf today has an approximate alcohol content of 0.5 percent.

30. Deuteronomy 11:13, 14 NLT
31. I Timothy 5:23
32. Psych Science 9/03

Chapter 2: Jesus Drank

A friend of mine has a Ph.D. in Greek and has taught Biblical Greek to Roman Catholic preseminarians at the Jesuit College in Philadelphia, Protestant seminarians at Eastern Baptist Theological Seminary (now Palmer Seminary), and secular doctoral students of Religion and Bible at Temple University. He summed up the beliefs of many Christians, especially Christians of the southern part of the United States and the "Bible Belt," this way:

"Specifically, Jesus drank alcoholic wine. Catholics, Eastern Orthodox Christians, and most Protestant denominations take this for granted. A few fundamentalist Protestant groups say he drank only unfermented grape juice. This is not based on any reasonable, scholarly interpretation of the Greek New Testament. These sincere Christians are afraid of their own vulnerability to Demon Rum if they permit themselves to drink even a little wine in moderation, afraid that soon they would be drinking too much and getting drunk. So they twist the Greek language to claim that the Bible says Jesus drank only grape juice, and all alcohol is evil, and we must never drink any of it. If this helps keep some of them from being drunkards, I am happy that their bad Greek and bad theology is doing them some good. But they are just plain wrong about Jesus' drinking habits. Jesus drank wine with alcohol in it, and served it to others, and asked that others drink it in memory of him."

I was born in Louisiana and raised in Florida near the Alabama line. The *traditional guidelines* of the Protestant church I attended as a child and young adult taught that drinking any kind, or any amount, of alcoholic beverage was a sin. And it didn't stop there; I was also taught to believe that going to the theater, bowling lanes, and to dances were sins.

Because I was raised in the southern part of the United States, I can tell you that many Southerners are ignorant about what the Bible actually says (I won't comment about any other regions of the world). Recently, in my hometown, I had a conversation with a man who refused to believe that Noah took fourteen reindeer on the ark. Even though I gave him the scripture reference,[33] he refused the thought of it. While he was sincere in his own belief, he was sincerely wrong. Moreover, he was opposed to seeking the facts.

---

33. Genesis 7:2

> **The Growing Season in Israel**
>
> Like most other food products in Palestine, grapes can only be grown during certain times of the year. In July, grapes, figs, and olives begin to ripen. During August, grapes ripen quickly and must be harvested. During September, farmers finish producing their wine, raisins, and syrup from their grape harvest. Usually around the end of September the first rains come after the long summer drought.
>
> During the time of Christ, the wine was stored in a variety of containers: bags made of leather, clay pots, and wooden barrels to mention a few. The stored wine allowed the farmer to have plenty of wine for the rest of the year, whether for his own personal use or for commerce.

The moderate use of wine is mentioned in a positive way throughout scripture. Moderation is the essential element to reaping the health benefits associated with the consumption of red wine. Drinking in excess has a direct toxic effect on the heart and other organs. Many strong recommendations against drinking alcoholic beverages in excess are given throughout the scriptures.[34] One that should be thoughtfully considered says that wine, by its very nature, draws a person into excess and leads them astray.[35] Failing to recognize alcohol as a powerful drug that creates a strong addiction is foolish.

A Gray Area

Long before the days of Prohibition, many United States Christians concluded that the consumption of alcoholic beverages was "sinful." Yet, in many countries outside the United States, Bible-believing Christians have no problem with the moderate consumption of wine and other alcoholic beverages.

Things that once were considered "sin" in many American churches are now often regarded as acceptable. It hasn't been too long since many Christian groups condemned others for going to the theater,

---

34. Proverbs 20:1; 21:17; 23:20–21; 23:32–34; Isaiah 28:1–8; Ephesians 5:18; I Timothy 3:3 & 8; Titus 1:7; 2:3; I Peter 4:3
35. Proverbs 20:1

owning a television set, going to the bowling lanes, investing in the stock market, listening to secular music, and surfing the Internet. Today, many of those same organizations use television, radio, and the Internet to broadcast their message, while their youth groups visit the theater and the bowling lanes on Friday nights.

There is a common thread that runs through these activities: Like many others, they are not discussed in the scripture. They are "gray" areas. These activities often tend to be associated with things that are inappropriate, lead a person into defined sins, and into social contact with people who are careless about the matters of the Lord. The problem occurs when godly people decide that these activities are counterproductive in their lives and label them as "sins."

For example, the game of billiards (commonly referred to as "pool") originated in northern Europe during the fifteenth century. Pool soon became the game of choice in taverns and pubs. The patrons of taverns and pubs tend to have some common characteristics: careless regard for family responsibility, drunkenness, profanity, sexual immorality, disregard for proper rest and nutrition, etc. This often leads to tardiness and low productivity at work, absence from worship and family devotions, irritability when faced with the routine duties of life, or the tendency to spend money on themselves while others have their basic food, clothing, and medical needs unmet. Furthermore, drunkenness often ceases to be rewarding and tends to become compulsive and obsessive.

But what does that have to do with a gray area? Since pool tables have a history of being associated with the activities mentioned above, many churches disallow the playing of pool and some will even go as far as to call it sin. This is about as silly as claiming that Acts 2:1 describes 120 people being packed into a Honda Accord.

Occasionally, you will hear somebody condemning the consumption of alcoholic beverages and citing I Corinthians 6:19 as their defense. "Do you not know that your body is a Temple of the Holy Spirit...?"[36] However, if you read the prior verse, you will discover that the writer was speaking about sexual immorality, not consumption of wine, being

---

36. NKJ

a sin against your body. This is an example of manipulating the scripture to validate your own "rules." More often than not, the person doing the manipulating is judging other people and is in error.

In the scripture, alcohol abuse is considered to be a sin and should be of substantial concern to Christians and non-Christians alike. However, this concern shouldn't lead to the judgment and condemnation of those who are users and not abusers.

Nazarite priests, who had made a vow to God, were prohibited from drinking wine and other alcoholic beverages.[37] However, once the vow had been fulfilled, the Nazarite was permitted to resume drinking wine.[38] Furthermore, if somebody wants to make the claim that Christians shouldn't drink wine, based on the analogy of the Nazarite vow, they must also condemn getting a haircut.

Some people interpret King James's use of the words "liquor of grapes"[39] to mean grape juice. However, the king may have been a little creative in his use of English during the translation of this verse. The Septuagint does not use the phrase "liquor of grapes." It instead states "... and whatever is made of the grape he shall not drink." It goes on to say, "Neither shall he eat fresh grapes or raisins." The use of the word "fresh" demonstrates that the writers during antiquity had the vocabulary to describe fresh squeezed (unfermented) grape juice, yet it is not used.

A Party Life

This chapter isn't an endorsement to live a party lifestyle. The message is clear: Drunkenness is sin and separates a person from God's kingdom.[40] Practically speaking, drunkards make lousy witnesses. And do you know anybody who encourages their children to be drunkards? Probably not. Neither does God. And being a "lush" is to live in willful sin and willful sin moves a person out from the blessing that comes from obeying Christ.

---

37. Numbers 6:3–5
38. Numbers 6:20
39. Phrase used in Numbers 6:3 KJV
40. I Corinthians 6:10

Living according to the scriptures leads to freedom, peace, and salvation. Living out from under the umbrella of God's blessing removes the Lord's protection over your family, health, peace, finances, and so forth. Want to be unstable? A party lifestyle leads to instability in all areas of your life. While the Bible does not condemn the moderate drinking of wine, the scriptures clearly condemn drunkenness and enslavement to alcohol. Old Testament law required that gluttons and drunks be stoned to death.[41] Proverbs says, "Wine and beer make people loud and uncontrolled; it is not wise to get drunk on them."[42] It goes on to say, "Whoever loves wine...will never be rich."[43] At times, there may seem to be exceptions to these scriptures but, in the end, the scriptures prevail.

The scriptures mentioned above are significant in that they confirm that the term wine could not mean grape juice. Why would the Bible condemn the excess drinking of grape juice, right? Moreover, you cannot become drunk with it, or get addicted to it. The bottom line is that if you want to stick with the argument that wine is grape juice, the negative statements in the scripture work to your disadvantage.

If all drinkers limited themselves to one glass of wine or a single drink a day, we wouldn't need as many law enforcement officers, cardiologists, liver specialists, mental health professionals, and substance abuse counselors. But not everyone who likes to drink alcohol stops at just one drink. While many people drink in moderation, some don't. Problem drinking affects not just the drinkers themselves but often their families, friends, and communities.

Even moderate drinking carries some risks. Alcohol usually disrupts restful sleep patterns if consumed within three hours of bedtime. Its ability to cloud judgment is legendary. Alcohol interacts in potentially dangerous ways with a variety of medications, including acetaminophen, antidepressants, anticonvulsants, painkillers, and sedatives. It is especially addictive for people with a family history of alcoholism.

---

41. Deuteronomy 21:20
42. Proverbs 20:1 NCV
43. Proverbs 21:17 NCV

God Views Wine as a Blessing

A lack of drinking wine is viewed as the Lord's wrath and judgment.[44] On the other hand, its provision is viewed as a blessing from the Lord: "May God always give you plenty of dew (rain) for healthy crops and good harvests of grain and wine."[45] The blessing continues, "If you carefully obey all the commands I am giving you today, and if you love the Lord your God with all your heart and soul, and if you worship him, then he will send the rains in their proper seasons so you can harvest crops of grain, grapes for wine, and olives for oil. He will give you lush pastureland for your cattle to graze in, and you yourselves will have plenty to eat."[46] Further examples where the provision of wine is viewed as a blessing from the Lord can be found throughout the Bible.[47]

One surprising statement (posted at the beginning of this chapter) allows for the unbridled use of tithe[48] money to purchase alcoholic drinks: "... Then exchange your tithe for silver, and take the silver with you and go to the place where the Lord your God will choose. Use the silver to buy whatever you like: cattle, sheep, wine, or other fermented drink, or anything you wish. Then you and your household shall eat there in the presence of the Lord your God and rejoice."[49] This scripture stands alone to vanquish all arguments regarding whether the wine mentioned in the Bible contained alcohol.

Aside from biblical teaching, the Mishnah (the oldest post-biblical recording of Jewish oral law created from a collection of historical works between 1200 B.C. and 200 A.D.) instructs the Jews to have four cups of wine during the Passover celebration meal. Christ and the disciples had two or more cups during the Last Supper.

---

44. In Jeremiah 48:33, Lamentations 2:12, Hosea 2:9 and Joel 1:10
45. Genesis 27:28 NLT
46. Deuteronomy 11:13–15 NLT
47. Deuteronomy 7:13; Jeremiah 31:12; Joel 2:19, 3:18; Amos 9:13, 14; Zechariah 9:16, 17
48. To avoid being guilty of robbing God, 10% of your income (a "tithe") is to be paid to the church - See I Corinthians 16:1,2; Hebrews 7:1–10; Malachi 3:8
49. Deuteronomy 14:25&26 NIV

Before you start spending your tithe money on wine, or anything else, notice that this statement was intended only for those who lived a great distance away and would have encountered undue hardship in their attempt to transport ten percent of their annual harvest to the place God chose.

The scriptures clearly show that wine is, more often than not, associated with the blessings of God. This leaves one to consider why so many Christians condemn the moderate consumption of wine and proclaim judgment and condemnation on those who partake. If you listen to them, you may be left to feel that the God they worship is opposed to music, dance, and wine. However, David was a skilled musician and danced in worship, the key word being "worship." I feel that God might actually want us to enjoy our life!

While one person may choose not to drink wine and another may partake, we shouldn't condemn or judge others for their choice. The best example of this is the difference between John the Baptist and Jesus Christ: John abstained from drinking wine[50] while Christ did not. Luke records Christ's words as he speaks to the Pharisees, "John the Baptist came and did not eat bread or drink wine, and you say, 'He has a demon in him.' The Son of Man came eating and drinking, and you say, 'Look at him! He eats too much and drinks too much wine, and he is a friend of tax collectors and sinners!'"[51]

Christ was certainly not a drunkard. Neither was he a glutton or obese (as are so many U. S. Christians today). But he did eat food and drink wine. When Christ made this statement[52] above he was denouncing the Pharisees and the lawyers for their stubbornness, their rejection of Christ as the Son of God, their disinterest in the good news, and their rejection of John the Baptist as a prophet.

Jesus was saying to the Temple leadership, "If somebody lives in the desert, choosing not to eat or drink, you call that person crazy. If another person chooses to eat, drink, and visit friends and neighbors, you call him a glutton, winebibber, and friend of notorious sinners."

---

50. Luke 1:15
51. Luke 7:33, 34 NCV
52. Luke 7:33, 34

Jesus Drank, Judas Repented and God Divorced His Bride

It seems Christ was also saying, because we're not saying and doing what you think we should, and we aren't part of your religious organization (kind of rhymes with denomination, doesn't it?), we're not accepted by you.

Not much has changed in 2000 years. In fact, if Christ had been born thirty years ago and started his ministry today, it's safe to presume that the religious leaders of *this century* would reject him.

Can you imagine the news article, "Man Claiming to be the Son of God Visits New York City!... His 'Miracle' crusade is attracting thousands of sick and diseased seeking prayer and healing. Thousands of sick and infirmed are leaving hospitals to join lines of people that stretch for miles. Local religious leaders question the 'No name preacher from Mississippi.'"

Millions would attend his healing services and there would be no end to the blogs debating the "outrageous" claims of being born of a virgin, and being God in the flesh. The knees of many religious leaders would knock together in fear as they contemplated the effect of his popularity on their ministry and finances.

Back to the point: If Christ had been drinking grape juice, it would have been difficult for the Pharisees to refer to him as a "winebibber." Christ chose to drink wine; John the Baptist chose to abstain. Christ explains the difference between himself and John the Baptist, making the point that their individual choices in this matter did not constitute "biblical guidelines."

We should look to the scriptures as our primary guidelines regarding our eating and drinking practices in public, in the company of other Christians, and in private. Here are the highlights from one of scriptures' most famous writers:

"One man's faith allows him to eat everything, but another man, whose faith is weak, eats only vegetables. The man who eats everything must not look down on him who does not, and the man who does not eat everything must not condemn the man who does, for God has accepted him."[53]

---

53. Romans 14:2, 3 NIV

If God accepts us, why shouldn't we use more common sense on these kinds of matters? And why do some people think they are better than they are? As I recall, the scriptures say we will all stand before God to be judged. And during the judging, I don't think anybody will be "perfect enough" so as to say to others, "See! I told you so."

For that reason we should stop judging each other. We must make up our minds not to do nothing that will make other Christians sin. I am in the Lord Jesus, and I know that there is no food that is wrong to eat. But if a person believes something is wrong, that thing is wrong for him.

If you hurt your brother or sister's faith because of something you eat, you are not really following the way of love. Do not destroy someone's faith by eating food he thinks is wrong, because Christ died for him. Do not allow what you think is good to become what others say is evil. In the kingdom of God, eating and drinking are not important. The important things are living right with God, peace, and joy in the Holy Spirit. Anyone who serves Christ by living this way is pleasing God and will be accepted by other people....So let us try to do what makes peace and helps one another.[54]

Wine, according to the scriptures, is a blessing from the Lord and something to be enjoyed in moderation. It is also a double-edged sword in that it is very addictive and is easily abused. However, those who choose to enjoy in moderation shouldn't be judged by those who choose to abstain.

The Significance of Using Wine during Communion

Please take your time reading the next five paragraphs. Slow down. Digest each sentence. Ponder. It lays a solid foundation for the next topic. A very important topic.

---

54. Romans 14:10, 13–22 NCV

Some feel that the transformation of grape juice into wine is significant and the "alcoholic glorification" is symbolic. They feel that in the same way that grape juice gives way to the yeast (the active agent responsible for the transformation) and becomes the wine of blessing, the Old Covenant gives way to the New Covenant. Ironically, pasteurization interrupts the God-ordained process of fermentation by killing the agent of that transformation. Grape juice is dead, but wine has passed from death to new life through fermentation.

In scripture, wine is a symbol of Christ's blood and the new life that he gave us. It is symbolic of the blood that flowed from Christ's body as the religious crowd crushed out his life, terminating the Old Covenant between God and man, and launching the New Covenant.

The fruit of the vine that was used during the Last Supper was wine, not grape juice. Grapes were harvested and stored during the months of August and September. Unfermented grape juice would have been unavailable in ancient Palestine in the spring of the year, since fresh grapes begin fermenting within minutes after crushing.

Jesus spoke of "the cup" as being filled with "the fruit of the vine,"[55] which designated that wine was partaken at the Passover and on the evening of the Sabbath. The apostles taught the use of wine in communion, as we can see from the fact that some members of the congregation actually became "drunk" at the celebration of the Lord's Supper.[56]

Along with the discovery of pasteurization, a tradition of using grape juice during communion evolved, and that's what it is: a recent, man-made tradition, not a biblical teaching. Traditions often find their foundation in the gray area where they, more often than not, become the "rules" of those who desire to enforce their traditions on others.

---

55. Matthew 26:29
56. I Corinthians 11:21

Chapter 2: Jesus Drank

Christ Received the Wine

Within the four different accounts of the crucifixion in the Gospels, you will find that Christ was offered wine twice. Contrary to what many people are led to believe, in neither case was the wine offered as sympathy or for comfort, "... I looked for some to take pity, but there was none; and for comforters, but I found none."[57] Both incidents were a fulfillment of prophecy in the narrative of Christ's work on Calvary.

Let me explain. In the first incident, soon after he arrived at Calvary, the wine offered to Christ was a mixture of wine and a bitter painkiller called gall,[58] which he refused. The sedative-laced wine was offered to crucifixion victims because it made the soldier's job easier. It was a form of anesthesia and served as a means to more easily subdue the victim during the horribly painful event of nailing the spikes through their wrists and feet. It is reasonable to conclude that the soldiers, who had beat Christ all night, had not suddenly become compassionate and full of mercy, offering him a cup of wine to help alleviate his suffering. It was a matter of protocol. It may not be unreasonable to conclude that Christ rejected the wine because it was laced with the deadly painkiller. He had foretold[59] that nobody would take his life, but rather he would willingly give his life.

The second incident was Christ's' reception of a wine-filled sponge and is a significant occurrence during the crucifixion. Only a few moments before Christ gave up his life he said, "I am thirsty," obviously suggesting that somebody give him a drink.[60] Keep in mind that Christ was extremely dehydrated at this point. Due to the violent beatings, which lasted most of the night, he had lost an enormous amount of blood and vital body fluids.

Upon hearing his request, someone brought more wine (without gall mixed into it) on a sponge attached to the end of a stick. The sponge was lifted to his lips, and Christ received the wine.[61] He immediately "gave up his spirit."[62]

---

57. Psalms 69:20 KJV
58. Matthew 27:34
59. John 10:18
60. John 19:28 NIV
61. Psalms 69:21; John 19:30 NIV
62. John 19:30 NIV

Some Southerners would argue that Christ was given vinegar. In the four different accounts of these incidents, Mark 15:36, is the only place where, in the Majority Text Greek manuscript, the word vinegar is used. However, "vinegar" means "sour wine." Could it be that Christ received the wine as a fulfillment of His prophecy given during the Last Supper? Did "kingdom power" come to the earth when he received the fruit of the vine? Let's find out.

The Fruit of the Vine: The Sign that the Kingdom of God Had Come

During the Last Supper, Christ referred to the wine as his blood and made a very profound statement, "For I tell you I will not drink again of the fruit of the vine until the kingdom of God comes."[63]

When would this "drink" be taken? Let's take a close look at a literal translation of the scriptures. Several hours prior to his death, Christ said that he would not drink of the fruit of the vine until the kingdom of God came. So Christ is saying that the next time he drinks the fruit of the vine, the kingdom of God would come. Hanging on the cross, Christ was moments away from giving up his life when he makes a statement: "I am thirsty."[64] Were these words merely a request for a drink, or was it time for the kingdom of God to come?

Prior to the death of Christ, the earth was under the complete control of Satan.[65] As he drew his last breath on the cross, the Bible records that Christ received the wine[66] and made his final and famous statement, "It is finished."

At the moment when Christ exhaled his last breath, the kingdom of God literally came, crushing the kingdom of darkness. With a thunder that resonated throughout the planet, Satan immediately lost his power

---

63. Luke 22:18 NIV
64. John 19:28 NIV
65. Matthew 4:9
66. John 19:30

over the earth. The kingdom of God rolled in and Christ was given unrestricted authority and absolute power, both in heaven and on earth.[67]

Symbolically, the Temple veil represented the separation that existed between God and man. The Jewish historian Josephus described the veil as being four inches thick and woven together so that it would have been impossible for two teams of horses (a team connected at opposing ends) to pull it apart.

The earth quaked, rocks split, light from the sun was extinguished, darkness covered the whole land, and the veil in the Temple was ripped in half, from top to bottom. Notice that it wasn't ripped from the bottom upward, as if done by men. Only an act of God could've ripped this four-inch-thick, woven curtain in half. The Temple veil hung from the sixty-foot-high ceiling and separated the Holy Place from the Holy of Holies.

When Christ's blood was poured out, and his body torn open as a sacrifice for our sins, Christ opened for us, through the curtain of his body (like the veil), unlimited access to God for Jews and Gentiles alike. Christ became the new, living veil. The Temple veil was now an unnecessary relic of an Old Covenant and it appears that God himself tore it in half!

God showed up. These earth-shaking events were part of the formal announcement that the Old Covenant was fulfilled and a New Covenant would govern.

---

67. Matthew 28:18

3 Judas Repented

"About the time of the end, a body of men will be raised up, who will turn their attention to the prophecies, and insist upon their literal interpretation in the midst of much clamor and opposition."

Sir Isaac Newton

The Monkees

During the 1960s, the four members of the rock band "The Monkees," performed a weekly television program that was aired on Saturday mornings. The band members were shown singing and playing all kinds of musical instruments. What's interesting to note is that none of them actually played a single musical instrument. All the music heard on the program came from a "hidden band" in the background.

A few years into their success, the members of The Monkees demanded the opportunity to learn and actually play their own musical instruments. However, they were met with great failure, marking the end of their careers in television. They were true "rock 'n' roll" impostors.

So how about Judas? Was he an impostor or was he, like many of us who started out with good intentions, only to make a mistake along the way? To find the answers to these questions let's start by asking, "What do the scriptures actually tell us about Judas?"

If I could point to a passage in the Bible that says, "Judas repented," you'd want to know about it, wouldn't you? If there were a passage where Judas confessed his sin publicly, you'd probably want to know about that one too, wouldn't you?

And if the scriptures clearly stated, "Judas repented" and "He confessed his sins," while Christ was standing in the room listening, then there would be solid ground for asking, "Would Christ have forgiven him?"

They're simple questions. Do you wish the answers were just as simple? Well, they are. Matthew 27:3–4 KJV says:

"Then Judas, which had betrayed him, when he saw that he [Christ] was condemned, repented himself, and brought again the thirty pieces of silver to the chief priests and elders, saying, I have sinned in that I have betrayed the innocent blood."

We've all heard the phrase, "Put your money where your mouth is." Matthew records that Judas repented, confessed his sin publicly, and spontaneously threw the money back. If Judas were an impostor, perhaps he would've just smiled and walked out of the room with his bag of silver. However, his actions seem to be those of a repentant man, not an unrepentant man.

As you read through the pages of this chapter you'll discover many things that may surprise you, two of which are:

- Christ promised Judas a throne in heaven.

- Christ was standing in the room where Judas repented of his sin and threw the money down.

These and many other significant events involving Judas will be discussed and reckoned within the pages ahead.

The Case against Judas

Epoxy adhesives come in two separate tubes. The two substances have no adhesive qualities apart from one another. However, when you mix the two, a chemical reaction occurs and, within moments, the two become one and create a strong, permanent, hard adhesive. Once epoxy is mixed, you only have a few moments to place it where you want it.

My friend Craig shared this analogy between the hardening of epoxy and the hardening of the heart to explain what may have been the plight of Judas:

"Symbolically, there's a form of spiritual epoxy. The two parts are made up of

a. willful, continuous sin, and

b. ignoring the ensuing convictions in their conscience (also referred to as the conviction of the Holy Spirit).

Together, these two form a spiritual condition known as 'hardening of the heart.' When a person continues in willful sin, and ignores their conscience, layers and layers of 'spiritual epoxy' cover their heart. Eventually, the heart becomes 'hardened' and that person no longer hears their conscience or feels conviction for sin."

Just days before his death, two women poured expensive perfumes and ointments (each worth a year's wages) on Christ on two separate occasions. It appears that all of the disciples disdained the apparent waste,[68] saying, "Why wasn't this perfume sold and the money given to the poor?" On the second occasion, Judas, treasurer of the group, was specifically outspoken about the waste,[69] Christ answered, "When she poured this perfume on my body, she did it to prepare me for burial."[70]

Perhaps this mention of "burial" caused Judas to realize that Christ *was* going to die soon. If that's the case, Judas is the only one who understood. Perhaps Judas, knowing that Christ was to be taken seriously, realized that Christ's income would dry up soon and decided to line his pockets one last time. Perhaps he was assuming Christ

---

68. Matthew 26:8; John 12:5
69. John 12:4, 5
70. Matthew 26:12; Mark 14:8; John 12:7

would escape from his captors as he had done so many times before[71] and viewed this as an opportunity to make some "fast money." Let's face it, Judas had watched Christ escape like modern day David Copperfield, walk on water, heal the blind, raise the dead, and feed thousands from one measly sack lunch. Roman guards submitted to him.[72] It's entirely possible that Judas may have been absolutely convinced that there was no chance in this world that anybody could capture or harm Christ.

These kinds of scenarios cannot be discounted because we do not know the tone of the writers, the intents of the hearts of those involved, neither do we know all of the events that occurred or what was said by everybody. Also keep in mind that, although the twenty-seven books of the New Testament have been proven completely reliable, they are only copies of copies. There are no known original copies of any books in the New Testament.

Whatever the thought process or motivation for his actions, Judas was headed straight into the history books for committing the most famous treason in all of history.

Luke says, "Then Satan entered Judas, ...,"[73] which simply means Judas submitted to the temptation to betray Christ. Perhaps the heart of Judas became more hardened each time he ignored his convictions and stole from the treasury. The point here is that If we willfully continue in sin, our hearts become hardened, which leads to an irreparable state. Hebrews 10:26 NIV says, "If we deliberately keep on sinning after we have received the knowledge of the truth, no sacrifice for sins is left,..." Again, each time Judas ignored his conscience and stole money from the treasury, he was turning back to his old nature and hardening his heart.

In a well-furnished kitchen there are not only crystal goblets and silver platters, but waste cans and compost buckets. There are also some containers used to serve fine meals and others to take out the garbage."[74] Similarly, there are some people that are predestined as vessels of honor and some as vessels of dishonor.[75]

---

71. John 10:39; 7:30, 44; Mark 12; 12; Luke 20:19; Matthew 21:46
72. John 7:44–46
73. Luke 22:3
74. II Timothy 2:20 The Message

Consider these startling examples; Rebekah gave birth to twin boys. Long before the twins were born or had done anything good or bad, God said of them, "Jacob I love, but Esau I hated."[76] Did you catch that? *God said*, " ...Esau I hated." This could lead some to ask, "Why does God blame us?" The answer may be in the book of Romans: "Shall what is formed say to him who formed it, 'Why did you make me like this?' Does not the potter have the right to make out of the same lump of clay some pottery for noble purposes and some for common use?"[77]

Pharaoh is an example of where God raised up a person to accomplish his own infinite purpose: "For the Scripture says to Pharaoh: 'I raised you up for this very purpose, ...'" [78] And Pharaoh resisted God to the point of his own death. However, the story may seem unfair when you read that God said, "... I will harden Pharaoh's heart..."[79] In this case, for his own infinite purpose God hardened the heart of Pharaoh who was predestined for his time and place in history. God's not fair; He's just.

Now, let me go on record: The debate regarding predestination is unsolvable and a mystery that cannot be solved in this life. Why? Because the finite mind of man cannot understand the infinite thoughts of God.[80] Before he was born, Judas was predestined to be the traitor in this theater of events. Is this unfair? Is God in contempt? Of course not. Somebody had to do what Judas did. And Judas was the person Christ chose. It could've just as easily been you or I. And Christ knew beforehand that Judas would betray him. Again, the mind of God is infinite. Predestination is infinite—that's why it's impossible to understand. A finite mind cannot grasp an infinite thought.

Regarding Judas, Christ said, "... Woe to that man who betrays the Son of Man! It would be better for him if he had not been born."[81] While praying for his disciples just hours before the crucifixion, Christ went on to say, "While I was with them, I protected them and kept them safe by that name you gave me. None has been lost except the one doomed

---

75. Romans 8:29–30; 9:21
76. Romans 9:13 NIV
77. Romans 9:19–21
78. Romans 9:17 NIV
79. Exodus 7:3
80. Isaiah 55:8, 9
81. Matthew 26:24 NIV

to destruction so that the scripture would be fulfilled."[82] It's easy to perceive these as words of anger, but could Christ have been using a regretful tone when he spoke? Of course. Consider it written this way: "Woe (which denotes intense *sorrow* or *grief*) for the man who betrays me! It would have been so much better if he had not been born. I've protected all of these men and they are safe, except the one predestined to fulfill the scriptures and who will, after which, commit suicide."

The case *against* Judas has been taught for centuries. But that doesn't mean it's the truth. Remember, almost all of the books in every Christian bookstore say two of all the animals went on the ark. Before he was born, Judas was predestined to be the traitor in this theater of events. And is this unfair? Is God in contempt? Of course not. God knew beforehand that Judas would betray him. What our human mind does not, and cannot understand is that God is infinite. Predestination is infinite. That's why it's hard (if not impossible) to teach or understand. Again, a finite mind cannot grasp an infinite thought.

Was grace available to Judas? Did Judas repent? Clearly, Pharaoh didn't. If Judas repented publicly of his sin, would Christ forgive him? Could grace cover his sin? Let's take a closer look at the answers to these questions.

Why All the Drama?

Have you ever wondered why Christ's closest friends abandoned him during his last night on earth? Were the events of Christ's final evening of life random or were they planned hundreds of years in advance? Was there a specific purpose for each scene that unfolded that evening? One thing is certain: The events weren't a surprise to Christ. He knew what was coming and why. Hundreds of years before Christ came, the prophets had written the final hours of Christ into the history books.

---

82. John 17:12 NIV

Perhaps the script could have been written differently, and the New Covenant ushered in with less drama. But this is not what God wanted. The prophets could have written the prophecies so that spies, working for the chief priests, planned his arrest,[83] but this is not what God wanted. They could have prophesied that Roman soldiers would arrest him as he and the twelve disciples walked openly through the streets of Jerusalem. But that isn't what God told them to write.

That would have been easy. Why did things have to get so dramatic? Why did there have to be conspiracy, abandonment, betrayals, suicide, and murder in the story that would ultimately split history into two eras, B.C. and A.D.? Were the events merely coincidental or did each one of the final twenty-four hours before the crucifixion have its own divine purpose? Although we do not get to know all of the answers in this life, two things are certain; God had a plan and purpose for every event and God loves drama.

During his greatest hour of need, Christ's closest friends deserted him and ran for safety. But after the resurrection they never walked away from him again. They were firsthand witnesses to the miracles, crucifixion, and the resurrection. And a few days later, when the risen Christ stepped through the wall into their boarded up room, he clearly defined their purpose in life: Take the good news to the ends of the earth. And because they would not betray him again, many died a martyr's death.

But for what good purpose would the prophets write Judas into this script? Why did it have to get that ugly? Why did a personal crime of such outrageous magnitude have to occur at this pivotal moment in human history? Why betrayal by a friend? Perhaps this event is a pivotal story within the greater story. Could it have been planned to stand as an example of the incomprehensible ability of Christ to forgive? Not a parable about forgiveness, but the world's greatest, real-life example of forgiveness?

Was the repentance of Judas merely a regret, as suggest? Was there no hope for Judas? Was he condemned for eternity or could he have found grace in the eyes of God before he died? The scriptures record that Judas repented, confessed his sin, and gave the money back.

---

83. Luke 20:20

Here's the big question: What greater trophy could Christ give to us to demonstrate his forgiveness than to forgive Judas and record his story in the Bible? I can't think of none other than my own sin.

Silver Screams

"Wherever your treasure is, there your heart and thoughts will also be."[84]

What people say is one thing. What they do is another matter. If you want an inside view of a person's character, look at how they use their money. A quick scroll through a person's reveals a lot about what the person values.

John the Baptist clearly explains that proof is required to validate repentance. Something of great value must be given. This discourages mere profession or outward show, "Therefore bear fruits worthy of repentance."[85] So, can the giving of one's substance be a "fruit" of repentance? Absolutely! In fact Moses explained that God demanded it.[86]

In the Old Testament, giving money to God was one of the requirements to make atonement for sins. Every person, rich or poor, was required to give a "ransom" of a half shekel for his or her soul. Their obedience also served to protect their health and well-being. And while the giving of their substance did not actually redeem their souls, their faith and obedience enabled redemption. Obedience matters!

In the parable of the rich young ruler, Christ said the only thing that kept the young man from being perfect was the act of giving money.[87] Keeping the commandments would lead to eternal life; giving away everything would do even more—it would lead to perfection. When Zacchaeus stood before the Lord, the scriptures record only one thing that he said: "I will give half my wealth to the poor, Lord, and if I have

---

84. Luke 12:34 NLT
85. Matthew 3:8 NKJ
86. Exodus 30:11–16
87. Matthew 19:21

overcharged people on their taxes, I will give them back four times as much!" By the way, in that day, this was the restitution required for a sheep thief.[88]

Zacchaeus' words represented a heart-changed repentance, and he backed them up with his eagerness to return money he had obtained deceitfully. Only then, after Zacchaeus responded with a "fruit" of repentance, did Christ say, "Salvation has come to this house today."[89]

After lying and deceiving his father and stealing from his brother, Jacob (whose name was later changed to Israel) offered his brother gifts of livestock and servants as part of his request for mercy and grace.[90] Perhaps Solomon had atonement in mind when he referred to money as a "defense."[91]

Ultimately, the greatest act of restitution known to mankind, the crucifixion of Christ and the shedding of his blood were offered as payment for our sin. When Zacchaeus and Judas offered to return the money deceitfully obtained, their actions represented the fruit of repentance.

Judas demonstrated repentance when he returned the money. To be sure, let's dig a little deeper.

It's All Greek

The Majority Text Greek manuscripts are the source for all modern versions of the New Testament. The earliest writings of the New Testament are only copies of the originals. There are no known copies of the original writings of any book in the New Testament. All we have are copies of copies. Although most of the copies are written in Greek, Matthew most likely wrote in Aramaic.

---

88. Exodus 22:1
89. Luke 19:8–9
90. Genesis 32:5
91. Ecclesiastes 7:12

Unlike Mark and Luke, Matthew was one of the twelve disciples. As the author, he was a firsthand witness to the events recorded in Matthew. Many theologians and experts agree that the book of Matthew may be the most reliable recording of the details of the life of Christ. Matthew was the only author to specify the exact amount of silver paid for the betrayal, and to record the episode of Judas' repentance and suicide.

Matthew was a tax collector by profession. He was considered strikingly candid by nature. He was an educated person whose career depended on his ability to examine and record the details of other people's financial affairs and business activities. The Roman government, one of the most organized, demanding government institutions in history, employed him.

Repented-Greek <u>Metameletheis</u>
Used only twice in the Bible in this exact spelling:

1. Matthew 21:29 Used by Christ while describing a change-of-heart and repentance with action.
2. Matthew 27:3 Used to describe Judas Iscariot.

In the Majority Text Greek manuscript, the exact spelling and use of the word *metameletheis* (English-repented in Matthew 27:3) is used only twice. It was used first by Christ to describe a young man in "The Parable of the Two Sons:"

Christ said, "What do you think? There was a man who had two sons. He went to the first and said, 'Son, go and work today in the vineyard.' 'I will not' he answered, but later he changed his mind [repented] and went. Then the father went to the other son and said the same thing. He answered, 'I will, sir,' but he did not go. Which of the two did what his father wanted? 'The first,' they answered."[92]

In the parable, the Majority Text Greek manuscript uses the word *metameletheis* for the word repented. The story describes repentance that includes:

---

92. Mathew 21:28–32 NIV

- Turning around and going in the opposite direction

- A change of heart

- Action

- Doing the will of the father

John the Baptist describes this kind of repentance as the "fruit of repentance." Moreover, as if to emphasize the meaning, Christ asks, which of the two sons...did what his father wanted?"

Other than this occurrence, the exact spelling of the word *metameletheis* is used only one other time: To describe the actions of Judas Iscariot. Here's how it reads:

"Then Judas, which had betrayed him, when he saw that he [Christ] was condemned, repented (*metameletheis*) himself, and brought again the thirty pieces of silver to the chief priests and elders saying, I have sinned in that I have betrayed the innocent blood."[93]

So, the question is: Did Judas repent? Did he do the will of the father? Often, scripture is clear and simple to understand. This may be one of those times. Christ defined the meaning of *metameletheis* in Matthew 21:29. Scripture reiterates the meaning with Judas.

Some say that Judas only felt regret. However, that appears inaccurate when Christ's specific use of the word is applied. You may want to use a Greek/English interlinear New Testament to do your own research and compare the words "repented" in both stories. A careful study of these two stories and the use of the word "repented" provides compelling evidence to the meaning. Judas' regret is punctuated with public confession and the immediate return of the money. Both actions meet the Biblical requirements for "fruit of repentance."

There are approximately ten Greek words for the English word "regret." With Matthews's knowledge and language skills, it is easy to argue that, if he had intended to describe Judas as only "regretful" he would

---

93. Matthew 27:3–4 KJV

have written it that way. Matthew clearly demonstrated in another passage[94] that he possessed all the vocabulary skills needed to describe impostors and those who were only sorrowful and regretful.

Audrey Conard's, The Fate of Judas[95] discusses Judas' role in the drama. Whether or not Judas repented (Conard also interprets different definitions of the word "metameletheis") is not as important as the returning of the 30 pieces of silver. First, the silver is in the hands of the priests, then Judas, then back to the priests again when Judas returns it. The priests ultimately take responsibility for the blood money because they are the last to touch it.

Conard explains, "It is a dramatic necessity on the story level that Judas hand over Jesus; on the level of Matthew's special agenda it is equally necessary that he hand over the money—and blame—to the chief priests." Consequently, it is necessary that Judas die so that he is not pointed to as the guilty party. As a result, Judas hangs himself after confessing his betrayal of innocent blood. Judas repented and the blame passed to the religious crowd.

The expression of "innocent blood" is where Conard's attention is most focused, not Judas' suicide. "It is not Judas who delivers Jesus to crucifixion; he has delivered Jesus to the chief priests and elders; they deliver him to Pilate. Pilate, on the other hand, also washes his hands of the innocent blood, and blames the people for his execution." As a result, Conard emphasizes that the chief priests and elders are responsible. The fact that the chief priests will not deposit the silver in the treasury displays their hypocrisy, knowing that it is innocent blood money, indeed. Knowing Christ was innocent, they did not repent, but rather demanded his death. No regret. No confession of sin. No renouncing of the blood money. And the story has a poetic, bizarre twist; the field they purchased with the money became the place where their own blood flowed thirty-five years later (via city sewer drains) when 1.1 million Jews were killed by the Romans. More about that later.

---

94. Matthew 19:22
95. Conard, Audrey. "The Fate of Judas: MT 27:3–10 (redactional analyses)."
    Toronto Journal of Theology. 7 (Fall 1991):158–168

Judas was a Jew raised near Jerusalem and most likely well-educated in Jewish law. He knew that he was guilty of shedding innocent blood and that there was no hope for him apart from his own death.[96] It appears Judas hung himself to do away with the curse brought upon him by the law.

Matthew lived and worked with Judas for three years and describes Judas' repentance as one characterized by a change of heart and a change in action. After witnessing the brutal death of Christ, it would seem unlikely that Matthew would have been lenient in his record of Judas' repentance and confession.

Judas Is Selected

Christ called Judas a friend.[97] It is important to realize that Christ selected Judas. Judas did not start a campaign seeking to be elected. Christ sought Judas knowing when, where, and how Judas would betray him.[98] Even as a man, Christ had an attribute of omniscience.

To be omniscient is to have all knowledge. Christ had knowledge of specific details about his own death,[99] he knew the specific details about a coin in a fish's mouth before the fish was caught,[100] he knew the private details of a woman's life of whom he'd never met,[101] and he also knew about Nathaniel before he met him.[102] Christ knew about many various things, including what people were thinking, and of events before they happened.[103]

Christ selected eleven leaders. He needed the twelfth to complete his entourage. He knew Judas was an essential element to the group—the last piece of the puzzle. If Judas had known what his future held, would

---

96. Numbers 35:33
97. Matthew 26:50
98. John 13:27, 28
99. Matthew 16:21; 20:18, 19
100. Matthew 17:27
101. John 4:16–19
102. John 1:47–49
103. John 18:4; Matthew 9:4; Luke 11:17; John 19:28

he have been so eager to sign up when Christ called him? Handpicked by Christ, Judas unknowingly stepped into place to become the world's most notorious traitor.

Would you submit your résumé for that position? A sane Judas Iscariot wouldn't have joined the group if Christ had described to him the events that would unfold. And Christ knew. Some argue that Christ was not omniscient; however, without any question, Christ knew about most events, things and people.[104] Did the Holy Spirit reveal only certain things to him? Who can know? One must also ask, "Is everything that was ever revealed to Christ by the Holy Spirit recorded in the Bible?" Of course not.

Christ knew the scriptures better than anybody. Hundreds of years before he was born, the pens of the prophets had written about the "Son of Perdition" and the pivotal turn of events that Judas would unleash. It's safe to say that Judas did not surprise Christ.

Christ's divine unwillingness to interfere with free will left the door open for Judas to do what he did. Some vessels God made for honor, and others for dishonor. Did Jesus work with Judas for three years, allow him to engage the most important event in history, and then send a repentant Judas to hell for eternity? Some may compare Judas to Pharaoh,[105] a valid comparison, except that there is no record of Pharaoh repenting, or confessing his sin.

Rarely does an unrepentant traitor confess. However, like the thief on the cross, Judas did. The thief on the cross, spontaneously and openly confessed his sin and defended Christ. Judas did the same. Pharoah did not.

Christ's sole purpose for coming to earth was to give his life as our "ransom money" for our sins, past, present, and future. Here's the big question: Even though Judas' actions were intentional, egregious, and unacceptable, if a truly broken and contrite Judas repented, would Christ forgive him?

---

104. John 4:17, 18; Luke 19:42–44
105. Romans 9:14–24

Imagine if Christ were sitting beside you today and you could look into his eyes and ask him, "Would you forgive Judas Iscariot if he asked for forgiveness?" What would his answer be? Would he say, "No?" Or would he be more likely to say, "Of course I would forgive him." I think perhaps the latter.

Our ways are not God's ways.[106] Scripture shows that God has never been entirely predictable. God may at times appear to even contradict what he has previously revealed.[107] However God never contradicts himself.[108] Whether he asks us to preach naked[109] or roast our food over a man's dung,[110] God is God, and does what he pleases! Psalms 115:3 says, "But our God is in heaven; He does whatever He pleases!" (NKJ)

We don't always understand what he does because of our limited, finite brains. Neither do we always receive an answer when we ask, "Why?" We don't get to say things like, "God, you can't give me a desire and expect me not to do it!" Or, "God, you can't create a place of punishment!" Or, "You can't make it that hard!" I love what L. Vernon McGee said, "This is God's universe. God does things His way. You may have a better way, *but you don't have a universe.*"

That just about sums it all up!

A Friend of Honor

Christ honored Judas. During a feast, it was Jewish custom and a symbol of honor for the host to personally give a portion to one of his guests. At the Last Supper, Jesus dipped a portion of bread into a dish and passed it to Judas. He prefaced the act with the words, "He who shares my bread has lifted up his heel against me."[111] With these words, Jesus quoted a passage which was written hundreds of years before.[112]

---

106. Isaiah 55:8
107. Acts 10:13–16
108. Num. 23:19
109. Isaiah 20:2–4
110. Ezekiel 4:12–15
111. John 13:18
112. Psalms 41:9 NASV

During the time of Christ, the Passover meal was eaten Roman-style, reclining at a three-sided table.[113] According to this arrangement, the guest of honor would have been to Jesus' left, and this would have been Judas. How do we know? Mark recorded that Judas[114] was the one who dipped the unleavened bread in the bowl with Jesus. The only persons who could share common eating vessels with the host were those to his right and left. One was identified as the "One whom Jesus loved," and was probably John. Since John asked Christ who would betray him, and since Jesus indicated that it was the one sitting next to him, this could only have been Judas.

Did Christ have compassion for Judas? Christ said, "It would have been better if you would have never been born." Were these words spoken in a condemning tone or could they have been spoken regretfully? In the same kind and forgiving tone that he spoke to the woman at the well, or the woman caught in adultery, he may have spoken to Judas. Christ loved Judas until the end, as the scriptures indicate.[115]

Christ and Judas worked together, side-by-side, for three years. Judas was there when Christ turned one "Two-piece Fish Combo Meal" into 5000 meals! How many times had Judas looked into the eyes of the blind as they watched their first sunset? How many times had Judas watched as Christ raised the dead?

Have you ever wondered why Judas instructed the Roman soldiers to take Christ away "safely?"[116] Would a completely self-centered Judas be concerned about Jesus' safety?[117] Famous Bible commentator Matthew Henry believes that Judas made full restitution for his mistake:

> First, He made restitution; He brought again the thirty pieces of silver to the chief priests, when they were all together publicly. Now the money burned in his conscience, and he was as sick of it as ever he had been fond of it. Note, that which is ill gotten, will never do good to those that get it. Jer. 13:10; Job 20:15. If he had repented, and brought the money back before he had betrayed

---

113. John 13:23
114. Mark 14:20
115. John 13:1
116. Mark 14:44
117. Matthew 27:3

Chapter 3: Judas Repented

Christ, he might have done it with comfort, then he had agreed while yet in the way; but now it was too late, now he cannot do it without horror, wishing 10000 times he had never meddled with it. See Jam. 5:3. He brought it again. Note, what is unjustly gotten, must not be kept; for that is a continuance in the sin by which it was got, and such an avowing of it as is not consistent with repentance. He brought it to those from whom he had it, to let them know that he repented his bargain. Note, Those who have served and hardened others in their sin, when God gives them repentance, should let them know it whose sins they have been partakers in, that it may be a means to bring them to repentance.

Secondly, He made confession (v. 4); I have sinned, in that I have betrayed innocent blood.

1. To the honor of Christ, he pronounces his blood innocent. If he had been guilty of any sinful practices, Judas, as his disciple, would certainly have know it, and, as his betrayer, would certainly have discovered it; but he, freely and without being urged to it, pronounces him innocent, to the face of those who had pronounced him guilty.

2. To his own shame, he confesses that he had sinned, in betraying this blood. He does not lay the blame on any one else; does not say, "You have sinned, in hiring me to do it," but takes it all to himself, "I have sinned, in doing it."

Matthew Henry does not credit Judas' confession as unto salvation. However, Judas' act of throwing silver coins away is a form of repentance. According to Jewish law, Judas' act was biblical. It also demonstrates a repentant man who realizes he's made a mistake and is making every possible effort to make restitution.

Keep in mind we have no reason to believe that the biblical record provides every word Judas said to the priests. He may have also said they were wrong to lead him to do what he did. And, alone in the night on the side of a cliff with a rope in his hands, who's to say he wasn't on his face, in the dirt, weeping, praying and pleading for forgiveness? These are only speculations, but one thing is certain: We do not know everything that was said and done by Judas, or anybody else in scripture.

Judas Was in the Building

During the time of Christ, the supreme court of appeals within the nation of Israel was a seventy-one-member Jewish Judicial Council known as the Sanhedrin. The Sanhedrin was the most powerful court in Israel. It was around nine o'clock in the evening when some or all of the members of the Sanhedrin gathered in their chamber. Soon thereafter, the cohort of soldiers delivered Christ into the chamber for this exceptional, unusual, and illegal midnight judicial hearing.

Jewish law specifically stated that, "Criminal processes can neither commence, nor terminate, but during the course of the day."[118] Neither could judgment be executed on the eve of the Sabbath or the eve of any festival. Strict Jewish laws also required that an attorney be present to represent the accused, and that the trials begin by presenting evidence that would acquit the accused, as opposed to evidence and testimony that made for the condemnation of the accused. Neither could a man's own testimony be used against him. At the mock trial of Christ, all of these laws were broken and not a single shred of evidence or testimony was sought that would acquit Him.

Perhaps the scene unfolded something like this: Before the trial began, Judas was given access to the chamber where the trial was to take place and he entered with Jesus.[119] Most have been taught and believe that this was John; however, no solid evidence exists to back up this *traditional* belief. Moreover, an event occurred in Acts that strongly suggests that the priests and high priests had never met John until some weeks after the resurrection when he and Peter went to speak with them.

The priests[120] "marveled" at the boldness of the "uneducated" and "unskilled" pair. The importance of this is the awareness to which the priests had come. After they "marveled," the original Greek text says, "… and they (the priests) recognized them that they were with Jesus." It appears as though it wasn't until this moment that the priests realized something like, "Oh, these two were followers of Jesus!" Prior to this meeting, Peter and John appear to be unknown to the priests.

---

118. The Talmud - Sanhedrin; C, IV, S.1
119. John 18:15
120. Acts 4:13

Tradition says that John often referred to himself as the disciple whom Christ loved. However, the scene in the chambers refers to "another disciple," not "the disciple who Christ loved." The Scripture only describes this person as one who was "known unto the high priest."[121] In light of this, it seems logical to conclude that this was someone other than John. More conclusively, the scriptures prove that Judas was the only one of the twelve who had ever met the priests. Furthermore, Judas is specifically named as being present in the chamber.[122]

So why would Judas be in the chamber? No doubt the priests were counting on him to testify against Christ.

Judas, seeing that Peter was outside in the cold, went outside, spoke to the doorkeeper, and brought Peter in. But why? Was Judas looking for moral support, or was he unknowingly doing the will of the father? I think the latter: Inside the chamber, Peter would be in direct eye contact with Christ when the cock crowed.[123]

One thing is certain; Judas went out of his way to bring Peter in to the meeting hall. And when the eyes of Christ met Peter's, Peter realized he had betrayed Christ—not once, not twice, but three times and the last time was with cursing and swearing.[124] Peter immediately ran from the Council chamber in tears.

When the trial began, Judas watched as the most powerful men in the country searched the crowd unsuccessfully for witnesses who would testify against Christ. Notice that Judas didn't testify against Christ. Things began to get ugly. Some of the guards spat in Christ's face. Another covered his head with a cloth sack. Some struck him repeatedly with the palms of their hands. The brutality had begun. And when the priests finished preparing for the execution, they interrupted the guards, proclaiming, "Bind him!" With that, Christ was readied for the walk to the Governor's mansion.

---

121. John 18:15
122. Matthew 27:3
123. Luke 22:61
124. Mark 14:71

At this time, it appears Judas realizes that Christ is not going to escape as he had done in the past. Realizing the horrible error of his judgment, and testifying to the innocence of Christ, Judas repents and erupts, "I have sinned, for I have betrayed an innocent man."[125]

Legally, Judas' words, "I have betrayed an innocent man," were a credible testimony and served as a direct witness of Christ's innocence and should have stopped the prosecution. However, the Sanhedrin had no intentions of setting Christ free. "What do we care? That's your problem," they retorted. It is then to his horror and disbelief that Judas slings the coins. And the sharp, ringing sound of thirty silver coins bouncing off of stone floors echoes through the chamber as Judas exits the building.

The Deal Was Sealed

Some who planned and participated in the murder of Christ had no problems living with their wicked deed. Their consciences had long been seared. However, following the resurrection of Christ, there was a great company of the priests who repented and became Christians.[126]

During the crucifixion, everyone witnessed a series of cataclysmic events and natural disasters. Darkness covered the earth from noon until 3 p.m.; the earth quaked under their feet; they watched as "... tombs broke open and the bodies of many holy people who had died were raised to life." Perhaps they looked like mummies, with rotting grave clothes hanging on them as they walked out of the tombs.[127] Could the scene have been more unbelievable?

It seems easy to conclude that at the sight of all this mayhem, some of the members of the Sanhedrin may have had second thoughts. Some of them may have looked around at one another thinking, "What in the world is going on?" I'll even go a little further and speculate that some,

---

125. Matthew 27:3 NLT
126. Acts 6:7
127. Matthew 27:53

upon realizing the error of their ways, considered how they might intercede and stop the crucifixion, unaware that Christ had already died.

However, as voting members of the highest court in the land, they would have known that any attempt to intercede in the crucifixion was impossible. Roman law forbade that a sentence be altered once it was pronounced. Their deal was sealed.

It is interesting to note that in the Coptic Orthodox Church, Pontius Pilate is commemorated as a saint. According to Coptic Orthodox tradition, Pilate secretly converted to Christianity sometime after the death of Christ, through the influence of his wife Claudia Procula. However, according to some Eastern Orthodox traditions, Pilate suffered deep regret for failing to intervene in the crucifixion of Christ and committed suicide. History provides very few substantiated details regarding the life of Pilate.

They Knew He Was Sent from God

The leaders of the Sanhedrin knew where Christ was from. A Jewish rabbi by the name of Nicodemus, a Pharisee and a voting member of the Sanhedrin, came to Christ privately during the night and admitted that they knew he had come from God.[128]

They had come to the right conclusion. However, their corporate denial of Christ wasn't because of disbelief in who Christ was—Christ just didn't fit the "profile" of their search. They were expecting a messiah who would be a military leader, to defeat the Romans and eliminate burdensome Roman taxation. They had a distorted image of the purpose of the Messiah. In their mind, the man Jesus Christ who preached "Love your neighbor as yourself" and "Pay unto Caesar that which is Caesar's" couldn't help them reach their personal goals. For this reason the Sanhedrin blindly rejected Christ as the Messiah.

---

128. John 3:1–2

Suicide

Some of you are probably familiar with golf's premier Professional Golfers' Association (PGA) tournament, The Masters. This annual tournament is played at the Augusta National Golf Club in Augusta, Georgia, which is generally regarded as the finest golf course in America. It is truly a masterpiece in the golf world.

Augusta National Golf Club is also one of the most difficult organizations in which to obtain membership. Just ask the National Council of Women's Organization Chair, Martha Burk, who took on the "men only" policy of the Augusta National Golf Club through the airwaves and print media in 2002–2003.

There are only about 300 members and membership is by invitation only. There is no application process. Acquiring a ticket to attend The Masters annual golf tournament is one of the hardest tasks in the world of spectator sport. The Augusta National Golf Club is truly an elite group!

The Bible has its own elite group. Within its sixty-six books, only twelve people ever earned the title, "Man of God." The prophet Samuel is one of those twelve. His approximate time of service as prophet for the nation of Israel was between 1100 and 1000 B.C. When he was a child, the Lord appeared to him and gave him his first prophetic message. The Lord stayed with him throughout his life and Samuel was known throughout the nation as God's prophet (a modern day Mother Teresa of sorts.)

Here are some of the qualifications to becoming a Man of God:

- Know the scriptures[129]

- Be perfect[130]

- Be fully equipped to do the works of Christ[131]

---

129. II Timothy 3:15–17
130. II Timothy 3:17
131. II Timothy 3:17

- Be inspired by the Holy Spirit[132]

- God makes himself known to him[133]

Little wonder it's a small group. Samuel, having a genuine desire for God, met these qualifications and was characterized by a lifetime of consistent obedience to God's will.

One of the main stories of the book of First Samuel is the rise and fall of the monarchy under King Saul. Unlike Samuel, Saul's life was characterized by inconsistency and disobedience to God and self-will. He did not have a heart for God and was dedicated primarily to himself, with occasional religiosity.

Because of Saul's disobedience, the spirit of the Lord left him. Not long after this, the prophet Samuel died. Saul had depended heavily on Samuel for divine wisdom and guidance. Without Samuel, Saul was "flying blind."

After Samuel's death, Israel's mortal enemy, the Philistines, gathered their army together and prepared an attack against Saul and the nation of Israel. When Saul saw the size of their army he was overwhelmed with fear.

Trembling, he repented and cried out to God for help, but God wouldn't answer. Like a drowning man, Saul was desperate. He made the decision to go to the neighboring city of Endor during the night, where he sought out the services of a notorious witch.

He explained to the witch that he wanted her to bring the prophet Samuel back from the dead. Since witchcraft was illegal in Israel, the witch was reluctant to help Saul. She eventually agreed, however, and the séance began. The prophet Samuel appeared and asked, "Why have you disturbed me by bringing me up?"[134]

After explaining his dilemma to Samuel, Saul asked for help. Samuel retorted, "Why ask me [to give you advice] if the Lord has left you and has become your enemy?"[135] What's more, the Lord will hand you and

---

132. II Timothy 3:16–17; Nehemiah 9:30; Numbers 11:16–29
133. Numbers 12:6; Ezekiel 3:17; Jeremiah 15:19
134. I Samuel 28:15 NKJV

the army of Israel over to the Philistines tomorrow, and you and your sons will be here with me."[136] And as fast as he had come, Samuel vanished and returned to his place in paradise.

The paradise to which Samuel returned was in a pre-New Testament place, not necessarily heaven. This paradise is where the righteous went before the resurrection of Christ.[137] This paradise, also referred to as Abraham's bosom, is where the beggar Lazarus was when the rich man looked up from hell, in torment, and cried, "... Father Abraham, have pity on me and send Lazarus to dip the tip of his finger in water and cool my tongue, because I am in agony in this fire."[138]

The next day, the Philistine army attacked, and Saul watched as all three of his sons were killed in battle. It was about this time that Saul was struck by an arrow and was mortally wounded.

Knowing that the Philistines would take him as a prisoner of war and torture him until he died, Saul made the decision to commit suicide and join Samuel and others in paradise.

Some feel that God would not allow the spirit of Samuel (or any other deceased person) to come back from the grave for any purpose. However, the scriptures prove differently. Christ took Peter, James, and John up a mountain where he transformed himself, "His face shone like the sun, and his garments became white as light." His spirit form temporarily broke through the veil of his humanity.[139]

Guess who else joined the party?, A couple of famous statesmen from centuries past: Moses and Elijah. Both appeared and began talking with Christ. As a point of interest, Moses and Elijah were also members of the Man of God group. (Perhaps one of the qualifications for being brought back from the grave is that you have to be a Man of God...but don't quote me on that.)

---

135. I Samuel 28:16 NLT
136. I Samuel 28:19 NLT
137. Matthew 12:40
138. Luke 16:24 NIV
139. Matthew 17:1–3 NIV

Chapter 3: Judas Repented

Let's flip back to the scene where Saul had engaged the services of the witch. During the séance, it seemed that the witch expected to see a ghost or a demon[140] because she was surprised and frightened when Samuel himself appeared. The Bible specifically says that Samuel came up. More significantly, during the séance the prophet Samuel accurately predicted the battle and the death of Saul and his sons. Demonic spirits could not have known these details.

Samuel, Saul, and the thief on the cross are three examples of those who went to the paradise when they died. Could it be possible that this is where Judas went when he committed suicide?

Some believe the commandment, "Thou shalt not kill" includes suicide. Perhaps the question, however, is, "Is murder an unpardonable sin?"

The problem with suicide is that one cannot repent because one is dead. Apparently, as we've seen in the case of Saul, God's grace can cover that too. Therefore, it would seem to be a given in cases of mental illness and such.

The word "murder" is used nine times in Scripture, yet it is not used during any of the four biblical incidents of suicide. Most dictionaries describe murder as the intentional, unlawful killing of one human being by another.

Most of us have been taught that there is no grace for those who have committed suicide. While most Westerners, including myself, don't view suicide as a noble resolution of a personal dilemma, many Japanese think the opposite, as did some ancient Romans.

While I do not condone suicide, there is little, if any, solid scriptural ground to support the teaching that suicide eternally dooms your soul. Suicide *can* be viewed as selfish. The person committing suicide is not "ending it all." They leave behind victims: children, moms, dads, wives, husbands, and others who are left to grieve and "pick up the pieces."

Some have been taught that suicide is an unpardonable sin. The Bible, however, defines an unpardonable sin as blasphemy against the Holy Spirit.[141] The Protestant Reformers, including Calvin, condemned

---

140. I Samuel 28:12

suicide as roundly as the established Catholic Church did, but held out the possibility of God treating suicide mercifully and permitting repentance. God can forgive you; however, it's a risky proposition to say the least, the final results of which are truly unknown.

If you were opposed to suicide, and your son, daughter, mother, father, spouse or close friend committed suicide, would you remain opposed to accepting the possibility that God's grace might have covered him or her? One can reason that suicide is objectively wrong because life is sacred, but is it unforgivable if we have accepted Christ the Son of God? We need only research and examine the story of King Saul to begin to discover the actual possibilities of God's grace regarding this sensitive issue. Could it be that perhaps even Judas, reeling in the pain and horror of his error, found grace?

A few years ago I set up a Living Trust as part of my estate planning. This trust will be used, instead of a will, to settle my estate at the time of my death. One of the documents included within the trust is a living will. In the event that I am injured or mentally incapacitated, and the attending physicians have placed me on an artificial life support system to keep me alive, the living will is an official written statement from me that instructs the physicians on whether to continue supporting my life.

Let's say that I have specified in my living will that I do not desire to be kept alive with life support. Therefore, I have chosen in advance to refuse life support in the event that it is needed.

Now, let's suppose I'm involved in an accident and the doctors deem it necessary to place me on life support. At some point the physicians, in accordance with my lawful prearranged request, are required to remove the machine that is keeping me alive.

Let's further suppose that, at that point, I die. Here's the question: Did I commit suicide? Furthermore, could this be interpreted as medically assisted suicide? Some may say yes, some say no, and that debate could go on for a long time.

---

141. Matthew 12:31–32

Chapter 3: Judas Repented

Another area of discussion could center on chemical imbalance. As an example, let's say that somebody is unable to obtain a refill of a prescription drug that keeps him or her "chemically balanced." Let's suppose that during the withdrawal period or at some point while they're not on the medication, the person becomes emotionally unstable and commits suicide. Does that person qualify for the grace and mercy of God?

A good friend of mine was taught in his Jesuit Catholic high school in 1951, when it was far less liberal than now, that most suicides were mentally sick and so not subjectively guilty of a serious sin and that for all we know Judas may be in heaven. The question may not necessarily be, "Is suicide right or wrong?" but rather, "Was the victim eligible for God's grace?"

If I have cancer, and my doctor advises me that chemotherapy and radiation will save my life, yet I refuse and end my life prematurely, is that suicide? I would say, "Of course not!" But didn't I make a deliberate choice to end my life? What if I refused the medical treatment because my religion taught me that modern medicine and science are sinful and you are supposed to let God decide such things?

Who's right? Who's wrong? While such illustrations may seem ridiculous to some, there are millions of people who live in these circumstances. Perhaps suicide, or any method of death, is not the real question, but rather, "Are my sins forgiven? Will God judge me worthy of heaven? Will he say to me, 'Well done, good and faithful servant?'"

Even though all four accounts of suicide in the Bible included victims who were in the midst of substantial personal dilemmas (i.e. physical pain, overwhelming emotional grief, shock, horror and fear), the question remains: Does suicide doom your soul for eternity, no matter the circumstances?

The eternal consequence of the act of suicide cannot be known for certain and the risk seems far too great to take the chance of being lost for eternity. In the cases of Judas and King Saul, there is arguable scriptural evidence that both victims may have been rescued by Christ and entered the kingdom of heaven.

The disciples asked Christ, "Who in the world can be saved?" Christ answered and said, "Humanly speaking, it is impossible. But with God everything is possible."[142] Perhaps these words will offer hope to some who lost their loved ones to the tragedy of suicide. Moreover, in the next section, "Reserved Seating," we'll investigate a promise from Christ that adds even more substance to the hope of those who have lost loved ones to suicide.

If Judas could have been rescued, would Christ have saved him? Scripture records that Judas exited the mock trial of Christ and committed suicide. If the possibility exists that grace was not available to Judas, is the whole message of Christ weakened? If Christ forgave Judas Iscariot, that act would stand alone as the greatest and most compelling message of hope and forgiveness in all of scripture. Could there be any greater?

Reserved Seating

Luke recorded the first business meeting of the New Covenant church. The first order of business was to elect a replacement for Judas. Luke writes, "For he was numbered with us and had obtained part of this ministry... Judas by transgression fell, that he might go to his own place."[143] Luke not only affirms that Judas went to "his own place" but that he had obtained part of the ministry as well. Perhaps Matthew provides us with a glimpse of the "place" that Luke is speaking of.

Peter asked Christ, "... We've given up everything to follow you. What will we get out of it?" Jesus replied, "I assure you that when I, the Son of Man, sit upon my glorious throne in the kingdom, you who have been my followers will also sit on twelve thrones, judging the twelve tribes of Israel. And everyone who has given up houses or brothers or sisters or father or mother or children or property, for my sake, will receive a hundred times as much in return and will have eternal life.[144] Notice how Christ finishes this promise with a seemingly unrelated and

---

142. Matthew 19:25 NLT
143. Acts 1:17, 25 KJV
144. Matthew 19:27–29 NLT

Chapter 3: Judas Repented

perhaps even mysterious statement: "But many who are first, shall be last; and the last shall be first."[145] Let's take a closer look at the promise Christ makes to the disciples in this statement.

First, he makes the unconditional promise to each of the twelve, "You who have been my followers will also sit on twelve thrones, judging the twelve tribes of Israel." Christ did not make any exceptions to this promise, neither did he attempt to exclude Judas. Second, Christ promised each of the twelve who gave up any of their "stuff" (real estate, relationships, and so on) that it would be restored one hundred times over. Third, Christ promised everlasting life to each one of them and a throne from which to rule and reign with him eternally.

These promises must be given significant consideration. Christ keeps his promises. Let's take another look: Christ ends on a mysterious note when he promises, "... But many that are first shall be last; and the last shall be first."

It was not unusual for Christ to speak in parables and mysteries. Often the disciples had no idea what he was talking about. Could his words in this final declaration be one of those times? I have read Bible commentaries where scholars try to determine exactly what Christ meant when he said this, yet it is difficult to find any two commentaries that agree with each other. In fact, some commentators list as many as six different "ideas" as to how they felt the Scripture could be interpreted.

According to Matthew Henry, Christ had special favor for the original twelve;

> The disciples had followed Christ when the church was yet in the embryo state, when the gospel Temple was but in the framing, when they had more of the work and service of the apostles than of the dignity and power that belonged to their office. Now they followed Christ with constant fatigue, when few did; and therefore on them he will put particular marks of honour. Note, Christ hath special favour for those who begin early with him, who trust him

---

145. Matthew 19:30 KJV

further than they can see him, as they did who followed him in the regeneration (Matthew Henry Complete Commentary, comments regarding the book of Matthew, verse 28).

There is a large amount of non-literal, non-historical parable and allegory in the Bible.

Twentieth century theologian Finis Jennings Dake said, "Let it be remembered that the first and chief fundamental principle of (scripture) interpretation is to take everything as literal unless there is plain evidence that the language is figurative."[146]

In context, let's take a literal look at the statement, "But many that are first shall be last; and the last shall be first." Christ seems to be explaining who would be first, and who would be last "to take their throne in paradise."

If this is the intended, literal message and Judas found grace through repentance, does it stand to reason that Judas became the first disciple to join Christ in heaven? Was Judas the first to take his place (throne) in heaven? Stay with me. Examine the scriptures below, paying special attention to the plural and singular forms used:

- "But many [plural] that are first..." (Peter, Andrew, James and John were the first four disciples that Jesus chose.[147])

- "... shall be last;" (They were arguably some of the last disciples to die; therefore, the last to receive their promised thrones.)

- "... and the last " (Judas is listed as the final disciple that Christ chose.[148])

- "... shall be first." (Judas was the first disciple to die.)

---

146. Dake's Annotated Reference Bible, page 7, note "L"
147. Matthew 10:2
148. Matthew 10:4

Whether or not this is what Christ meant when he added that phrase at the end of his promise may remain a mystery. But three things are for certain: Christ knew how the life of Judas was going to end; Christ knew that Judas would become history's most notorious traitor; and Christ excluded none as he made the promise.[149]

Before you unbuckle your seatbelt and bail out, consider this: Christ often went against tradition and from accepted religious dogma. He was notorious for surprising his listeners. And they often did not understand him at all. He was a rebel with a cause. Let's keep digging!

The Backward Redeemer

"My thoughts are completely different from yours, says the Lord. And my ways are far beyond anything you could imagine. For just as the heavens are higher than the earth, so are my ways higher than your ways and my thoughts higher than your thoughts."

Isaiah 55:8–9 NLT.

He's popular for doing things backwards. Perhaps it is just to see how we will respond and to test our faith and character. Case in point: the parable of the laborers in the vineyard.[150]

Here's another story that is sure to catch you by surprise. In Palestine, it was customary for those who had been hired first in the day to be first to receive their pay at the end of the day. They had been there longer and tradition mandated that they were first to be paid their earnings. But when Christ tells the story, he flips tradition and practical reasoning on its head. Here's a paraphrased version of the story:

Fatigued and sweaty, they'd been in the fields since 6 a.m. They'd worked straight through the heat of the midday sun. It would be a mild understatement to say that they were anxious to leave. Unfortunately, there was a delay. Confused, they watched and listened as the owner of the estate spoke.

---

149. Matthew 19:28
150. Matthew 20:1–16

The owner had begun calling names, but they were the wrong names. The workers stepping forward to collect their pay were workers who had been hired just a few minutes before quitting time. "This is not right," some grumbled impatiently.

Then, just so those who worked since daybreak could see and hear him, the owner of the vineyard counted out a full day's pay to those who had hardly worked an hour. With joy and excitement the now fully paid late-comers left the vineyard.

The others began to think, "Wow! This is great! If he paid those guys that much money, what's he going to do for us? We've hit the jackpot!"

However, when the owner began calling their names he only gave them the pay they'd agreed to at 6 a.m. The group begins to get hostile. "That's not right!" they exclaimed. "We've worked all day long, through the heat of the day, yet you've paid us the same amount as those who worked for only a few minutes! This isn't fair!"

The owner replied, "My friend, have I not paid you the wage that you and I agreed on? What business is it of yours what I do with my money? Are you angry because I have chosen to be generous? I have paid you what I owe you, now be on your way."

And then, once again, Christ makes the statement, "The last shall be first, and the first shall be last." Notice that every time Christ says this, he specifies that this is how the Kingdom of Heaven works.[151]

An infinite Kingdom of Heaven operates at a level that is higher than our human understanding.[152] Who can know it?

---

151. Matthew 19:30, Matthew 20:16, Luke 13:30
152. Isaiah 55:9

Chapter 3: Judas Repented

God's Not Fair. Ever.

God is a just God. God is not fair, and nothing in the scriptures describes God as being fair. Jeremiah called God the habitation of justice! In the book of John, Christ spoke of himself saying, "My judgment is just." Solomon wrote in Proverbs, "To do justice...is more acceptable to the Lord than sacrifice."

There is a vast difference between justice and fairness. For example, fairness says that as an American citizen, I have been given the right by the United States Supreme Court to abort my baby if I choose to do so. On the other hand, justice says, "Don't commit murder."

Just because an organization has given you its legal approval to do something does not necessarily make the action just. Sadaam Hussein gave his blessing to those who were willing to murder Jews. Was that justice? Of course not. The fact that our government has legalized the murder of unborn children does not mean that justice has been served.

Most would say, "Let Judas burn!" Yet, God says, "My ways are not your ways. I'm a God of mercy and grace. I will serve my justice and my righteousness."

Mercy is different from grace. Grace is receiving what you do not deserve. Mercy is not receiving what you do deserve. None of us have earned God's grace, yet most hope that we will receive it. So I'll ask again: If God's grace and mercy can cover a sinner like you and I, can it cover Judas Iscariot?

One of the most famous serial killers of all time was Ted Bundy. Bundy was arrested while pumping gas at the corner of Palafox and Cervantes streets in Pensacola, Florida. The clean-cut, handsome serial killer confessed to twenty-eight killings, but other estimates indicate he killed between thirty-three to one hundred female victims during the 1970s. According to Bundy, his descent into sexual assault and murder was born and fueled by an addiction to pornography.

On the last day of Bundy's life, Christian psychologist James Dobson interviewed him. This interview took place on Monday, January 23, 1989, at 2:30 p.m. at the Florida State Penitentiary in Starke, Florida. Bundy called Dobson and offered the interview with the understanding that it would be used to warn the public about the horrible pitfalls of pornography. Many suspect that he was making excuses for himself. Bundy was also working with law enforcement, using maps to show where he'd buried bodies all across the country. Bundy appeared to be doing the only things that could give any restitution for his crimes.

Dobson said that Bundy wept several times during the interview: "He expressed great regret, remorse for what he had done, for the families that were hurting." Bundy claimed to have confessed his sins, and received Christ as his savior and attempted to make restitution. He was executed at 7:15 a.m. the day after this interview.

So here's the question: Would Christ forgive Ted Bundy if he truly repented? Absolutely. The scriptures tell us that we can't "out-sin" God's grace. But, we're talking about Ted Bundy! We don't want to forgive him! Fairness screams, "Let him burn." Grace, however, says, "But because of his great love for us, God, who is rich in mercy, made us alive with Christ even when we were dead in transgressions—it is by grace you have been saved."[153]

God's grace is bigger than the sins of Ted Bundy. Will we, can we, forgive those who have wounded us? What if your wife or daughter had died at the hands of Ted Bundy? Forgiveness is not easy. It cost God the life of His Son! For most of us, forgiving others will be our greatest challenge in life.

Christ knew that somebody had to do what Judas did. Grace reasons, "There is grace for the Judas Iscariots of this world." As I said earlier, if Judas' sin hadn't killed Christ, mine would have.

God Was Pleased with the Death of Christ

But it was the Lord's good plan to crush him and fill him with grief. Yet when his life is made an offering for sin, he will have a multitude of children, many heirs. He will enjoy a long life, and the Lord's plan will prosper in his hands. When he sees all that is accomplished by his anguish, he will be satisfied. And because of what he has experienced,

---

153. Ephesians 2:4, 5 NIV

my righteous servant will make it possible for many to be counted righteous, for he will bear all their sins. I will give him the honors of one who is mighty and great, because he exposed himself to death. He was counted among those who were sinners. He bore the sins of many and interceded for sinners.

Isaiah 53:10–12 NLT.

As Judas darted out into the night from the room where they were having supper, Christ said, "God is glorified!"[154] Why? Because Christ knew that Judas would now start the wheels spinning at high speed. Meanwhile, the other eleven disciples are mostly, if not entirely, clueless about what was going on behind the scenes. With puzzled looks, some probably gazed through the doorway into the dark of night. They had no idea what had just happened.

Christ had saved his next words for this exact moment in time. They are perhaps some of the most important words ever spoken: "So now I'm giving you a new commandment: Love each other. Just as I have loved you, you should love each other. Your love for one another will prove to the world that you are my disciples."[155]

This is one of the most important commands that Christ gave to us. Christ didn't say, "Love the widows" or "Love those who hate you." No. Those commands had been given. Christ referred to this as a new commandment; its release was planned for this particular moment.

Soon, the whole world would know that one of Christ's own had defected. It would be "the talk of the town." The powerful and the homeless, the rich and the poor, would watch and wait to see if this "new religious" movement would self-destruct. Only one thing could keep the eleven from imploding: "Your love for one another will prove to the world that you are my disciples."

Would they have to love Judas when they finally discover the role he played? Absolutely. Did "Love one another" include loving Peter, to whom Christ had referred to as "Satan"[156] and who would betray Christ three times? Yes! Would it include the two nervy, rude, and impolite apostles James and John, nicknamed the Sons of Thunder for their

---

154. John 13:30–34
155. John 13:34, 35 NLT
156. Matthew 16:23

unbelievable self-centeredness?[157] Would "Love one another" include loving the large number of priests who repented shortly after the resurrection?[158] Yes to all the above.

In Nikos Kazantzakis' *The Greek Passion*,[159] the Turkish Muslim pasha says he doesn't need to guard his village against a band of refugee Greek Christians because "you will see how these Christians hate one another." Throughout the centuries the pasha's cynicism has often been more true than Christ's command.

Was the timing of the words of Christ a coincidence? Perhaps not. Christ knew the secret to holding our lives together: "Love one another." His timing of this announcement could not have found a better place in the drama unfolding that night. In the days ahead, their love for one another would be tested. First, the pride, self-centeredness and selfishness that did exist between them would be abated. Humility and love for one another would take its place. Each man would soon be looking at the other from a position of true empathy. Why? Even though Judas and Peter led the way, each and every disciple betrayed Christ that night.[160] In the weeks and months ahead, there appears to be no self-righteousness among them. Perhaps this "position of empathy" explains why you can find little, if any, condemnation of Judas in all of their historical writings.

Christ Forgives Judas

After nailing Christ's wrists and feet to the cross, the Roman soldiers stood the cross upright where it dropped into a hole. The cross stopped abruptly as it hit the stone bottom. Gravity caused the rusty, iron spikes to rip violently at the bone and flesh of Christ's wrists and feet. Pain so severe would have thrown most people into unconsciousness.

At that moment, Christ made the world-famous statement, "Father, forgive them, for they know not what they do."[161] I said Christ made the world-famous statement, "Father, forgive them, for they know not what

---

157. Mark 10:33–38
158. Acts 6:7
159. New York: Simon & Schuster, 1954
160. Mark 14:27–31

Chapter 3: Judas Repented

they do." After being physically abused all night, with his lifeblood flowing out of open wounds and in pain so severe it would bring the strongest man to his knees, the Son of God asked his father to forgive all of the people involved in this event.

When Christ prayed this, he was stating a matter of fact: The elders, chief priest, Pilate, Judas, the Roman soldiers, and the mob were all completely unaware of what they were actually doing. They were closing the door on the Old Covenant and giving birth to the New Covenant (New Testament). But Christ knew, and his first words were to beg the pardon of those involved. Would you expect any less from him?

He came for this purpose. There is no exclusion found in his prayer. He didn't say, "Father, except for the Sanhedrin and Judas who have willfully and spitefully set out to harm me, forgive everybody else involved." That's what most of us would have said. But Christ is grace. He is mercy. He is love. Ever offering to give to us what we don't deserve. Always desiring to withhold what we do deserve.

Could it be argued that only the self-righteous would deny to Judas the grace and forgiveness that was given to all that day? Who are we to deny Judas the same grace given to us?

Author Gary Amirault of TentMaker.org wrote a compelling article titled "Judas Iscariot-In Heaven or In Hell." The following is a short excerpt:

> To summarize, be careful where you place Judas. He did the will of the Father and fulfilled the scriptures. Peter, whom we all love, tried to prevent Jesus' crucifixion and was called "Satan" by our Lord. Peter, who was not mindful of the will of God, was restored. Was it not Jesus who said, "Anyone who does the will of my Father in heaven is my brother and sister and mother" (Matthew 12:50)! Be careful about placing Jesus' brother, Judas, in Christendom's "hell." One day you may have to look up to Judas, instead of looking down on him. Peter denied him three times in one night while Judas declared Jesus innocent in front of the High Priesthood. Judas had a very important job in the Kingdom of God. For three and one half years, as a Priest, he inspected the Lamb

---

161. Luke 23:34 KJV

of God as an unbiased man. He was not "one of them," a Galilean. He was the outsider. He did his job perfectly. If Judas really wanted to mess things up, he could have agreed with the High Priesthood and called Him a "blasphemer" who claimed to be the Son of God when He really wasn't. But Judas declared the Lamb spotless and unblemished, the Perfect Passover. Thank you, Judas, for not only being a hearer of the Word, but also a doer of the Word. Thank you, Judas, for giving the redemption money which purchased the Potter's field; a place for strangers in the land of Israel and the silver which speaks of the redemption of the family of Adam who sold himself as a slave to sin.

You may not like how Judas got that money, but you should rejoice in what it did for you. (Visit http://www.JudasRepented.com to read the article in its entirety.)

None of Them Is Lost

Have you ever talked to anyone who had just been told that he or she had only a few weeks to live? Have you ever listened to an interview of a death-row inmate a few hours before execution? In most sane cases, their comments are deeply thought out, sober, and sincere.

In the hours before Christ would be executed, Christ leaves us with some interesting words to consider regarding the disciples.[162] The following are excerpts from that prayer:

- They all belong to you

- I have given them eternal life

- They have received and kept the word of God

- Those that thou gavest me, I have kept: and none of them is lost but the son of perdition; that the scripture might be fulfilled

- You gave them to me

---

162. John 17:1–26

Chapter 3: Judas Repented

Christ said, "Those that thou gavest me, I have kept: and none of them is lost, but the son of perdition; that the scripture might be fulfilled."[163] At the time of this prayer Judas was lost, that the scriptures might be fulfilled. Did Judas stay lost? Who can know for certain? Moreover, aren't all Christians lost before they come to repentance? Does the promise made by Christ in Matthew 19:28 exclude Judas?

Later that night Judas repented and confessed his sins with Christ standing in the room. Christ heard Judas, just as he would listen to the confessions of the thief on the cross a few hours later. Some feel that Christ may have already been moved to the Governor's mansion for questioning. Wouldn't Christ have heard the voice of Judas when he cried out in repentance? Of course. Also remember that the events had been written centuries earlier. Besides, hearing across town was no problem for Christ. He hears from heaven when you cry out.

True repentance is always accompanied with its partner: humility. At perhaps the most embarrassing and devastating moment in his life, and without any hesitation or pride, Judas shouts an immediate and humble confession. Christ heard Judas' words of repentance, the tone of his voice, and only as Christ can, Christ knew the intents of his heart as Judas said, "I have sinned! I have betrayed an innocent man!" Christ knew the precise moment the silver would hit the floor,[164] the only outward sign of restitution that Judas could offer.

Judas made a conscious decision to commit a heinous crime. Only a few hours had passed since Christ said, "Yes, it would have been better, if he had never been born." Could it be that these words came from a heart of sorrow, grief and grace knowing the role that Judas would play? I hope so. Because if they did, there's hope for you and I.

Thieves Don't Give Back the Money

When does a thief give back money that he or she has stolen and hidden? More often than not, thieves don't return the money. Moreover, if they know they are going to be caught, they try to hide the

---

163. John 17:12
164. Matthew 27:5

money so they can recover it at a later date. Most criminals, if they have the time to hide it, will go to prison before they'll give the money back.

Judas did not get caught. Nobody walked up to him and said, "I know you were paid to give up the location of Christ." Rather, he comes forward and confesses his sin and volunteers the return of the money. It seems he makes every attempt available to stop the trial. He wants nothing to do with the event. No, Judas didn't "get caught" doing something wrong and then try to "cut a deal" with the authorities in hopes of obtaining a more lenient sentence. He did the opposite. He realized his awful mistake and repented, just as Matthew describes.

Judas truly repented in his heart of what he had done and then confessed. Moreover, would a man of only shallow regret commit suicide? A shallow, cold-hearted traitor would have moved on with his life and the money he had taken. The chief priest and others did just that. It would appear, however, that the guilt and shame were more than Judas could bear.

Judas was a thief. Christ knew it. Christ once asked the disciples, "Have I not chosen you and one of you is a thief?" Judas was the kind of guy who was always looking to make a "quick buck." That's what thieves do, right?

When Christ chose him, Judas' life would never be the same, but like most of us, he didn't become a perfect man. Judas, along with the other eleven, was given power over unclean spirits, to cast them out and to heal all manner of sickness and diseases.[165] Imagine that. Judas Iscariot praying for people; casting demons out of the possessed, praying for the sick, maimed, blind, and those with leprosy.

For three years Judas was a disciple and trusted friend of Christ. Psalms says, "Even my own familiar friend in whom I trusted, who ate my bread, has lifted up his heel against me."[166] The word "familiar" in the Hebrew means peace, prosperity, completeness. Judas and Jesus shared life as comrades[167] together before the crucifixion, and Judas'

---

165. Matthew 10:1
166. Psalms 41:9 NKJV
167. Matthew 26:50

role was vital for the redemption of mankind. Could Christ's love for Judas survive the betrayal? Should we hope so, since our own sin would have been enough to crucify him?

A Thieves' Paradise

Do you remember what the thief on the cross did to earn eternal life? In only a few seconds he found something that most of us struggle to find in a lifetime. If your answer is, "He believed" then you'd better keep looking. "...[E]ven the demons believe that—and shudder."[168] Belief alone is insufficient.

Here's a hint: He didn't need a "Super Size;" a small amount would do. During the last moments of his life, the *faith* of the thief in Christ as the Son of God made the difference. His *faith* alone secured his unconditional eternal salvation.

During an uneventful time in Israel's history, a man named Jabez prayed a short, simple prayer and gained the favor and blessings of God. That prayer has become quite popular in the modern world. "Oh, that you would bless me and enlarge my territory! Let your hand be with me, and keep me from harm so that I will be free from pain."[169] Short but effective. This too was the repentance of the thief. Just like most of us, he didn't try to clean up his act before he came to Christ. He probably wasn't very benevolent, supportive of charity, or involved in feeding starving children. Chances are good that he never bothered to give offerings to God or honor the Ten Commandments. He was a felon and probably a repeat offender. The guy was a notorious criminal and he was being crucified for it. And his time was running out quickly.

This thief may have been more intelligent than we've imagined. Why? He feared God,[170] rebuked the other thief for his lack of faith, confessed his sin and his wretched state, acknowledged responsibility for the crimes he had committed, respected the justice for those crimes, proclaimed the innocence of Christ, proclaimed Christ as Lord,

---

168. James 2:19 NIV
169. I Chronicles 4:10 NIV
170. Proverbs 9:10

professed faith in the eternal kingdom of Christ, and asked Christ for mercy and forgiveness. All of this in the span of about thirty seconds. That was faith. Brilliant faith. And God's grace covered him.

One of You Is a Devil

Whenever we talk about Judas, we have to look at these particular words of Christ: "Have not I chosen you twelve, and one of you is a devil?"[171] The Greek word, *diabolos*, means adversary, false accuser and slanderer. The original Greek can be more accurately translated this way: "Did I not choose you twelve, and one of you is an adversary?"

A few hours before the crucifixion, Christ said to Peter, "Get thee behind me, Satan [Greek, borrowed from Hebrew: Satanas meaning adversary]."[172] Obviously, in Christ's words this did not mean that Peter actually became Satan. The writer Luke also used the same Greek word while referring to Judas, "Then Satan entered Judas… "[173] In this instance, the reference to "Satan" entering into Judas simply means Judas became an adversary and submitted to Satan's temptation to betray Christ. Judas did not turn into Satan nor did Satan turn into Judas.

Christ most always reserved his harshest words for the religious crowd: the priests, elders, scribes and Pharisees. In contrast, Christ never cursed Judas, Peter, or any of his disciples. In fact, quite the opposite: Christ was especially caring toward Peter after the resurrection; and when Judas entered the garden of Gethsemane, Jesus called him "friend."[174]

---

171. John 6:70 KJV
172. Matthew 16:23
173. Luke 22:3 NKJ
174. Matthew 26:50

So When Did Peter Repent?

Peter was talking with Christ earlier in the evening before his capture and they had a conversation that went something like this: "If everybody else deserts you, Jesus, I won't." Jesus replied, "The truth is, Peter, this very night before the rooster crows at dawn you will deny me three times." Peter replied quickly, "I'll die first."[175]

Christ knew Peter better than Peter knew himself. Within a few hours, Peter and all of the other disciples had deserted Christ.[176] Peter's loud, public, under-oath betrayal of Jesus was a glaring contrast to the others who betrayed him in the garden. While the others avoided interrogation and remained silent, Peter's was a far more outspoken betrayal.

Peter betrayed Christ three times that evening. Yet, we have no record of a verbal repentance and public confession of sin. The Bible does not record that Peter repented or confessed his sin, yet without any hesitation, most (including myself) readily believe that he did. Peter went on to write at least two books in the New Testament and was a valiant apostle, dedicated missionary, and most probably a martyr for the cause of Christ.

Peter, one of the most colorful figures in scripture, was a man of God. After Christ ascended back to the Father, he didn't return to the fishing nets that he knew so well. He kept the faith and preached the saving grace of Christ for decades. Was Peter's betrayal less of a sin than that of Judas? Probably not. Could grace cover both Judas and Peter? Absolutely.

The Slave Trader

Can anybody exhaust God's grace? How about one of the world's most notorious slave traders? He was personally responsible for bringing literally tens of thousands of Africans to America against their will to be

---

175. Luke 22:33,34
176. Mark 14:50

sold as slaves. As a slave ship captain, John Newton[177] was regarded by his own crew as the most disgusting, profane, inhumane, blasphemous and wretched drunk alive.

Lindsay Terry writes of Newton, "It is reported that at times he was so wretched that even his crew regarded him as little more than an animal. Once he fell overboard and his ship's crew refused to drop a boat to him. Instead they speared him with a harpoon and dragged him back into the ship."

After Newton repented of the error of his ways, he spent the rest of his life writing songs and preaching about God's grace. He would go on to pen the words to one of the most famous songs in history, "Amazing Grace." Few could be more qualified to write it than a man who participated in the capture, persecution, slavery, and death of thousands.

As the Bible teaches, Newton believed that none could exhaust God's grace. If he were alive today, what message do you suppose would he preach about Judas Iscariot?

Impostor or Genuine Article

Christ summed up his entire message with "Love the Lord with all your heart, soul and mind...and love your neighbor as yourself. Everything in eternity hangs on these two commandments."[178]

Okay, loving God—that's no problem! But loving your "neighbor?" Why did he have to say that? Why not "Love your parents" or "Love your children?" Why, for goodness sake, did he have to say your "neighbor?"

It's no accident that Christ chose those words. With their barking dogs, noisy cars, unruly children, trashy lawns, and loud music, Christ knew that our neighbors would be our greatest challenge. Of course, as the

---

177. John Newton (July 24, 1725 - December 21, 1807) Anglican clergyman and
    former slaveship captain
178. Matthew 22:37–40 paraphrased

story of the Good Samaritan demonstrates, our neighbor is not just the guy next door, but all of mankind, even those from hated ethnic groups. Christ knew we would be making progress when we arrived at the place where we could truly love our neighbors.

It was his final road trip to Jerusalem. His evangelistic career was coming to an end. His final showdown with the enemy, the battle at the cross, wasn't something he was looking forward to. Then again, who would? Would you be excited to ride willingly into the hands of those who were going to beat you into a near unconscious state, nail you to a cross, spear your side and hang your bruised, bleeding body on display where your mother and friends would watch helplessly until you died?

At the end of that scene, his final prayer was not for safe passage, but for those who were abusing him: "Father forgive them...."

In order to be forgiven, we must forgive. Allow me to repeat: *In order to be forgiven, we must forgive.* If we do not forgive, then God will not forgive us.

After watching the crucifixion, John, the only disciple at the scene of the crime, summed it up: "If someone says, 'I love God,' and hates his brother, he is a liar; for he who does not love his brother whom he has seen, how can he love God whom he has not seen? And this commandment we have from him: that he who loves God must love his brother also."[179]

If you claim to love God, you must also love Judas. God intends the love of himself and the love of man to be inseparable parts. Otherwise, we do not have God's love.[180] Obedience to God's commands is the only "fruit" that shows our true love for Christ. Obedience is the substance of love; it's what separates an impostor from the genuine article.

Love your neighbor. Genuinely. That includes the person in the car in front of you who stops at the green light; the person in the grocery line ahead of you whose credit card isn't working; the server in the

---

179. I John 4:20–21 NKJ
180. I John 5:1–3

restaurant who forgets your dinnerware; the prodigals; the person on the back row who was unfaithful to their spouse; and the person who divorced you because you ran out of money;. They are your neighbors.

If Christ were walking the earth today, he'd probably be focused on healing those who are HIV positive. Perhaps Christ would use these famous words, "See, you are well again. Stop sinning or something worse may happen to you."[181]

When you begin to look at people through God's eyes, the way that God looks at them, then you are making progress. Making a dedicated effort to seek the lost and sick and share the good news of salvation is what Christ would do. When you and I can do this, then we have God's love. Anything less is, as the song says, "just fooling around."

The Verdict

While nobody can be one hundred percent certain about the fate of Judas Iscariot, one thing is certain: his fate is sealed, while yours is not. You have the opportunity to choose who you will serve, and in the words of Bob Dylan, "You're gonna serve somebody."

Almost without any exceptions, Christians who were reaching out to help other people founded all of the hospitals and orphanages in America. The same can be said of our Ivy League colleges and universities. They too were founded by Christians who were interested in educating America's children so they could further the good news of Christ. If you don't believe me, visit the "History" page at http://www.Yale.edu.

Writers like John Newton and the writers of the scriptures do not place Judas in a devil's hell. So who are we to do it? Who can be sure of the fate of Judas? If you can't out-sin God's grace, there's hope.

---

181. John 5:14 NIV

Christ died for every man, woman, and child. He loves you, and accepting him as your Savior is easier than you may think. Just remember the thief on the cross, who in about thirty seconds confessed that he was a sinner, recognized Christ as the Son of God, and asked for forgiveness (for which he was immediately granted).

"The Light of the World"

You may have seen the famous painting of Christ, portrayed standing at a door, titled "The Light of the World," by William Holman Hunt. "The Light of the World" is a sermon on canvas.

"The Light of the World" allegory Hunts' chosen for illustration, originates in the Book of Revelation, "Behold, I stand at the door and knock; if any man hear my voice and open the door, I will come in to him, and will sup with him, and he with me."[182]

On the head of Christ are two crowns: the earthly crown of his shame as well as his heavenly crown of glory. The robe is seamless, symbolizing the unbroken body of Christ.

He is holding the "lamp" of the Word. The cords of the lamp are twisted around Christ's wrist, exemplifying the bind that exists between him and the Church.

The door of the soul has been closed for a long time. Weeds have climbed where they could not had the door been kept open; briars flourish because the gardener has not come and fruit has fallen to the ground from the tree.

A bat hovers overhead—the bird of darkness, ruin and neglect. The ironwork is rusty and stained. Upon close examination you will notice the absence of a doorknob. The door can only be opened from the inside.

---

182. Revelation 3:20 KJV

The expression on the face of Christ seems sad, as if he has knocked and knocked in vain. It would appear, as indicated by his half-open hand and listening mannerism, he is waiting patiently and listening for someone to come.

X X X X X X X

If you haven't already done so, say a prayer of repentance today. He's knocking and waiting at your heart's door, but the knob is on your side of the door. It is up to you.[183]

"The Light of the World"
by William Holman Hunt

---

183. Revelation 3:20

4 God Divorced His Bride

Politics

A few miles south of Baghdad, Iraq, in the small village of Kifil, a cone-shaped monument towers above the rooftops of homes in the crowded residential area. Visible from several blocks away, the monument is actually the roof of a tomb. The tomb is the traditionally recognized burial place of the prophet Ezekiel.

During biblical times, the geographical land area (give or take a few hundred miles in any direction) of modern Iraq was referred to as Babylonia and its capital city as "Babylon." It was also referred to in Greek as Mesopotamia. As a point of interest, here are some popular biblical (all but one) events that have taken place in Babylonia/Iraq:

- The Tower of Babel was built in Babylonia[184]

- The creation of the different languages took place in Babylonia[185]

- Abraham was from Babylonia[186]

---

184. Genesis 11:1–4
185. Genesis 11:5–9
186. Genesis 11:31

- Jonah was swallowed by the whale before going to Nineveh, which was in Babylonia[187]

- Daniel was in the den of lions in Babylonia[188]

- Belshazzar, the King of Babylonia, saw the hand writing on the wall, in Babylonia[189]

- Three Hebrew young men, Shadrach, Meshach, and Abednego, were thrown into the fiery furnace in Babylonia[190]

- Ezekiel wrote the Book of Ezekiel while in Babylonia

- The book of Revelation speaks about Babylon[191]

- On March 20, 2003, the United States and the United Kingdom launched a military invasion on the nation of Iraq and took occupancy there

Ezekiel was a prisoner of war and one of three major biblical prophets. The Babylonian army invaded Israel around 620 B.C. During the siege, Ezekiel (along with many other Jewish leaders) was captured, taken prisoner, and carried away to Babylonia. While there, Ezekiel prophesied and warned Israel of her sin, rejection, and rebellion against God's word.

Ezekiel wasn't a coward. Neither would he have made a good politician. He didn't sugarcoat his words. Ezekiel described the harlotry and whoredoms of God's bride in explicit and vivid detail: "Yet she became more and more promiscuous as she recalled the days of her youth, when she was a prostitute in Egypt. There she lusted after her lovers, whose genitals were like those of donkeys and whose emission [semen] was like that of horses."[192]

---

187. Jonah 3
188. Daniel 6:16
189. Daniel 5:5
190. Daniel 3:20
191. Revelation 17 and 18
192. Ezekiel 23:19, 20 NIV

I want to make sure you caught that last part: Ezekiel said the Egyptian men were well-endowed. It appears the Israeli women liked this physical trait and kept going back to Egypt in pursuit of sex with the Egyptian men. While Israeli men were generally smelly, dirty sheep herders, farmers, and brickmakers, many of the ancient Egyptian men were modern day "Chippendales." Generally tall and slim, Egyptian men were famous for wearing rouge, cologne, nail polish, etc. And religious practices required the use of eye shadow from birth for both male and female citizens.

Additionally, good personal hygiene practices (i.e. daily bathing) were expected in ancient Egypt and these practices added to the reasons why the Israeli women loved Egyptian men.

Spiritual Adultery

Although Scripture records the sexual failures of numerous men and women, there are nonsexual sins that are more serious in the eyes of God, though they usually get less attention.[193] For instance, Christ was merciful and compassionate toward a woman caught in the act of adultery, but he condemned the attitudes of arrogance, self-righteousness, stubbornness and greed.

Spiritual adultery is condemned as equally as physical adultery—perhaps even more. It is spoken of as idolatry, covetousness, and apostasy.[194] Spiritual adultery is the common act of idolatry: loving the things of the world more than the things of God. Worldly goods include money, sexual sin, homes, or anything that we place our affections on more than our desire for Christ and holiness.

God considered Israel as his covenant wife and this is spelled out in scripture with "I am married unto you"[195] and "Your maker is your husband."[196] Even though she was unfaithful and continued in rebellion, God was faithful to his word, allowing her scores of opportunities to repent.[197] Of course, this is just a metaphor. Jesus is

---

193. Proverbs 6:16–19
194. Jeremiah 3:6, 8, 9; Ezekiel 16:32; Colossians 3:5; I Peter 4:3; Revelation 2:22
195. Jeremiah 3:14 KJV
196. Isaiah 54:5 NKJ

called a vine, a road, a shepherd, and an elevated bronze serpent. He is not these things. God is like a husband to Israel but he is not sexually fathering children as the pagans believed their gods did with human women.

Although called the chosen people of God, the scriptures imply that the people of Israel chased after and worshipped false gods such as Baal and Ashtoreth.[198] These pagan gods were worshipped with all forms of illicit sex and violence. Some of their priests and priestesses were male and female prostitutes. Israel was committing both spiritual and physical whoredom when they indulged in this idolatry.

It appears that God divorced Israel on the grounds of spiritual adultery. Although God hates divorce, the scriptures seem to say that the whoredom of his bride was continual and without repentance.[199] God sent Israel away with a divorce decree.[200] However, at a supposed later date most modern translations record that God says, "...I am your husband."[201] Assuming that the statements are chronologically accurate, this seems to imply that God did not divorce Israel. However, the Septuagint[202] reads, "Turn, ye children that have revolted, saith the Lord; for I will rule over you: and I will take you one of a city, and two of a family, and I will bring you into Sion [Zion]." God appears to be saying, "Repent and I will take you in like a family." He does not say that he is still her husband. The current translation issue most likely arises from 1611 A.D. when King James I of England translated his version of the Bible.

God's Divorce

"She saw that for all the adulteries of that faithless one, Israel, I had sent her away with a decree of divorce."[203] "Where is your mother's certificate of divorce with which I sent her away?"[204] The scriptures

---

197. Ezekiel 16:32
198. Judges 2:11–15
199. Ezekiel 16:15–41
200. Jeremiah 3:8
201. Jeremiah 3:14 NIV
202. The earliest Greek translation of the Jewish Scriptures/Old Testament translated between 300–200 B.C.
203. Jeremiah 3:8 RSV

seem clear that God divorced his bride due to harlotry (idolatry) and unfaithfulness to Him. Was this a complicated divorce? Very much so, and more complicated than most. God had two wives. Here's an abbreviated explanation.

In the Old Testament, God was married to Israel[205] and was considered the "husband God" of Israel.[206] Israel was divided and became two daughter kingdoms—the house of Israel and the house of Judah, the two wives of God.

God was the husband of both the house of Israel and the house of Judah.[207] However, his wives were not faithful.[208] Ezekiel further describes both wives as sisters and prostitutes, Aholah and Aholibah.

Aholah (Israel) represented Samaria, the capital of the northern kingdom. Aholibah (Judah) represented Jerusalem, the capital of the southern kingdom.[209] Samaria and Jerusalem, the kingdoms' capitals, lie about thirt-five miles apart.

Even though Aholibah was considered the more active prostitute of the two, God divorced Aholah (Israel) first.[210] God remained married to Aholibah and was tightly bound by the marriage covenant. The marriage with Aholibah could end only with the death of the husband,[211] who in this case was God.

The death of Christ, God incarnate, on the cross finalized the divorce from Aholibah. At the time of death, Aholibah (Jerusalem/Judah) was released from the Mosaic Law. The Old Covenant was fulfilled and a New Covenant began. The New Covenant was an open invitation for all to come, whether Jew or Gentile, and be part of the new bride of God by faith in Christ as the Son of God.

---

204. Isaiah 50:1 NIV
205. Exodus 19:4
206. Exodus 6:6–8
207. Jeremiah 31:32
208. Ezekiel 16:1–8
209. Ezekiel 23:1–20
210. Jeremiah 3:6–11
211. Romans 7:1

The Old Covenant could be compared to a very exclusive "club" where membership could only be obtained if you were a descendent of Judah or a convert. Hence, we have the tribe of Judah, which became known as Judaism and the Jewish culture.

The Mosaic Law had created a legalistic, imperfect, and Pharisaical institution—Judaism. However, Christ didn't come to destroy it but to fulfill and perfect it. This is why he said, "Do not think that I have come to abolish the Law or the Prophets; I have not come to abolish them but to fulfill them."[212] Christ came to remove the veil (wall) between God and man, so both Jews and Gentiles could have a one-on-one, direct relationship with God. Again, this is why God tore the Temple veil from top to bottom when Christ drew his last breath on the cross. When Christ died, it was the last blood offering required for the forgiveness of sin and a complete fulfillment of the Old Covenant.

With the death and resurrection of Christ, all were given equal access to the presence of God, a deal sealed for all of eternity compliments of the blood of Christ. As a result, every man, woman, and child can now approach God in prayer to worship and make their requests known. The scriptures indicate strongly that this privileged place is no longer reserved exclusively for the descendants of Judah.[213]

The divorce decree was given because God desired a new bride, a New Covenant and a relationship with you and me. However, he could not be married to both Judah (an Old Covenant relationship based on strict rules) and his new bride (a New Covenant relationship built upon love, forgiveness and grace) simultaneously. While speaking to a group of educators, Paul said:

> Do you not know, brothers—for I am speaking to men who know the law—that the law has authority over a man only as long as he lives? For example, by law a married woman is bound to her husband as long as he is alive, but if her husband dies, she is released from the law of marriage. So then, if she marries another man while her husband is still alive, she is called an adulteress. But if her husband dies, she is released from that law and is not an adulteress, even though she marries another man.[214]

---

212. Matthew 5:17
213. Galatians 3:21–28
214. Romans 7:1–3 NIV

God's specific grounds for his divorce from Israel can be found in Ezekiel.[215] Below are a few reasons referenced in Ezekiel for which God divorced his bride:

- Used their beauty and fame to increase their whoredoms

- Practiced pagan idol worship in many elegantly decorated indoor and outdoor brothels within the city

- Created gold and silver statues, fashioned in such a way as to have sex with them in a form of heathen worship

- Placed God's holy oil and incense before their idols

- Sacrificed the lives of their children with fire

- Considered their whoredom an insignificant and private affair

- Enjoyed sex with anybody who was interested

- Hired lovers to have sex with them

- Forgot the days when they were poor and naked and forgot how God rescued them and made them what they were

A Command to Marry a Prostitute

The Lord commanded Hosea to marry a woman who was radically sexually immoral. This was a woman with children as a result of her prostitution.[216] Hosea stayed faithful to her and did not forsake her, even though she left him and continued her extremely immoral lifestyle, living in adultery.[217] The Lord never instructed Hosea to divorce his adulterous wife. Moreover, even though there was no repentance indicated on her part, Hosea was told to love her, bless her abundantly and reaffirm the marriage commitment between them.[218]

---

215. Ezekiel 16:15–43
216. Hosea 1:2, 3
217. Hosea 3:1
218. Hosea 3:1–3

The story of Hosea is an example of how God loved his bride. It parallels God's dealings with Israel. It also serves as an example of how we are to love our spouse in this present age.

The Stoning of God's Bride

It was a cool Sunday morning and a dry, gentle breeze blew across the faces of those lined along the caravan road between Bethany and Jerusalem. They waved palm branches and sang praises as Christ, riding on a donkey, passed by. However, the same crowd would soon be screaming and demanding his death sentence.

He rides through the last dip in the dusty road before the steep walk up the side of the Mount of Olives. Once at the summit, a full and fabulous view of Jerusalem built on its own small mountain, bursts into view. With the Temple Mount in the foreground, the city rises up. Herod's palace crowns the top. Christ has a bird's-eye view of the city. Thousands of people are busy taking care of their day-to-day business, completely unaware that God is there (all too often true of us in our daily lives).

Tears begin to stream from his eyes and down his cheeks as he speaks, "I wish you knew today what would bring you peace. But now it is hidden from you. The time is coming when your enemies will build a wall around you and will hold you in on all sides. They will destroy you and all your people, and not one stone will be left on another. All this will happen because you did not recognize the time when God came to save you."[219]

Christ further described how before the second coming of Christ, the nation of Israel, as well as the Temple, would be destroyed.[220] The stoning of the bride could not be avoided. Those who had acknowledged, yet later rejected Christ as the Messiah, were on a collision course with tribulation: "For then there will be great tribulation,

---

219. Luke 19:41–44 NCV
220. Luke 21:12–24; Matthew 23:36–39; Matthew 24

such as has not been since the beginning of the world until this time, no, nor ever shall be."[221] Christ goes on to say, "This generation shall not pass till all these things be fulfilled."[222]

Under Old Testament law, if a man and a woman were found in adultery, their punishment was death by stoning. Moreover, if a woman was found guilty of losing her virginity before marriage, the elders of the city (religious, civic and/or judicial leaders) took her to her father's front door and stoned her to death. Helpless to intervene, this was also the father's punishment for allowing his daughter to lose her virginity. Shortly stated from the Old Testament law, there was little tolerance for adultery, and a woman's life pivoted on preserving her virginity until she was married.[223]

Warnings had been issued. Prophecies had been given. Twice, Ezekiel was inspired by God to describe how Israel would be stoned to death for her unrepentant sins of adultery, murder, idolatry, child sacrifice and so on.[224]

After the crucifixion and resurrection of Jesus, as widows of God the Jews refused to believe that the Mosaic Law was completely fulfilled in Christ. Ironically, the Mosaic laws they refused to vanquish became the same laws by which many were judged when the Romans stoned and burned the city: "From the sky huge hailstones of about a hundred pounds each fell upon men.... They will bring her to ruin and leave her naked; they will eat her flesh and burn her with fire."[225]

The mode of death was stoning for a common adulteress[226] and the mode for a priest's daughter was death by fire. The apostate portion of the house of Judah was both, so she was stoned and burned.[227] But was it just another stoning, or was it the Great Tribulation that Christ spoke of?[228]

---

221. Matthew 24:21 NKJV
222. Matthew 24:34 KJV
223. Deuteronomy 22:20–22
224. Ezekiel 23:37–49 and Ezekiel 16:35–41
225. Revelation 17:16; 16:21 NIV
226. Leviticus 20:1
227. Revelation 16:21; Revelation 17:16; 18:8
228. Matthew 24:21

The Great Tribulation

Most Christians have heard of the "Great Tribulation." Many books have been written and movies produced about a "silent rapture" that marks its beginning. The teaching is a common part of the the eschatology of Dispensationalism. I myself was raised in a church that taught Dispensationalism.

The earliest roots of Dispensationalism sprung up about 150 years ago. Prior to this, Christians throughout history taught that the Great Tribulation was the destruction of Jerusalem by the Roman army in 70 A.D. I believe the latter is true. Let's take a look at a few reasons to question the teaching of Dispensationalism.

Born out of the restless religious environment in England and Ireland in the 1820s, Dispensationalism took root in the teachings of John Nelson Darby (1800–1882).

Dispensationalism maintains four basic principles:

1. There is a distinction between Israel and the church.
2. There is a distinction between the Law and Grace.
3. The New Testament covenant perfected the Old Testament covenant.
4. The "Rapture" of the church at Christ's coming "in the air"[229] precedes the second coming of Christ by seven years of tribulation.

Dispensationalism teaches that the "Rapture" takes place when Christ appears in the heavens along with all of the saints who previously died. As Christ descends, but does not touch the earth, the faithful who are alive on the earth at this time will be taken up to meet the Lord in the air, or "raptured."

---

229. 1 Thessalonians 4:17

According to the Dispensationalists, once the rapture takes place, a seven-year period called the "Great Tribulation" will begin. During these seven years, many on the earth will perish. At the end of the seven years, a vast coalition army from several nations, led by the Antichrist, will mobilize at Armageddon against Jerusalem.

Armageddon is the name given to the site of the final battle between the forces of good and evil. The site is a valley plain called Megiddo, which is the location of several decisive battles during ancient times. At this time when Jerusalem is surrounded, Christ returns the second time to deliver Israel and punish the nations for their persecution of Israel. The battle of Armageddon will last less than twenty-four hours.[230]

However, there are different ideas among Dispensationalists. Some believe that the first coming of Christ will happen at the beginning of the Tribulation; others believe it will happen during the middle of the Tribulation, and some believe that will happen after the Tribulation.

Is the "Great Tribulation" a future or past event? I tend to favor the literal interpretation of the Scriptures, which teaches that the Great Tribulation Christ spoke about[231] occurred in 70 A.D. However, I agree with the Dispensationalists that Christ will return to earth again as Armageddon unfolds. And according to the Word, this time when Christ descends from heaven, he will land on the Mount of Olives in Jerusalem, splitting the mountain in half.[232]

When will that happen? The time is sooner than it's ever been. There's never been a time in modern history when powerful nations were more able to annihilate the Jewish nation-state of Israel. Soon, Iran will have the ability to deploy nuclear weapons. Nothing should alarm you more than a radical, extremist Muslim nation with nuclear weapon capabilities. And Iran seems steadfast to keep its *recent* promise to wipe Israel "off of the map."

---

230. Zechariah 14:1–7
231. Matthew 24; Luke 21:12–24
232. Zechariah 14:1–9

As is the case with most Christian traditions, Dispensationalists have a piece of the truth. But can anybody really have future world events completely figured out? Of course not. Christ himself said that even he didn't know the time of his return.[233] And it is safe to say that nobody is going to get to heaven and be able to say, "See, I told you."

Though popular in recent years, Dispensational eschatology can get complicated. On the subject of the Great Tribulation, I tend to accept Christ's words literally. That's not to say that I am right; I just try to keep it simple. Besides, you can take the books of Daniel, Ezekiel, Isaiah, Zechariah, Matthew, Luke and Revelation, mix them together and create unlimited variations of end-time scenarios. .

Many believe the events that occurred during the Roman-Jewish war were actually the events of the Great Tribulation mentioned by Christ. The reasonableness of the claim is substantial and backed up with in-depth Scripture references.

Tribulation Gold

In 66 A.D., there was a vast store of gold hidden inside the Temple in Jerusalem. Nero, the Emperor of Rome, had known about it for years. When the demand for more gold (taxes) was finally made, the flickering flames of the Roman-Jewish War exploded. Does this sound reminiscent of a certain 1773 December tea party in Boston?

The Jewish revolt was about taxes and government power. Not only did Rome lust for the treasure, they needed it. Rome had burned, and financial deficits had grown to overwhelming proportions. Moreover, it was essential for Rome to officially crush the revolt for the purpose of sending a message to the rest of the world that any future tax revolts would be met with brute force.

---

233. Matthew 24:36

Legend has it that, near the end of the siege, a misguided flaming Roman arrow found its way onto the Temple roof, and this "Roman Candle" started a blaze. According to witnesses, the blaze soon spread across the city. Whatever the cause, the Temple burned and prophecy was fulfilled.[234]

At daybreak, narrow ribbons of smoke from the charred rubble streamed up into the clear, crisp blue sky. As the smoldering ash cooled, the Romans made a startling discovery: The cache of gold inside the Temple was a much larger treasure than they had ever imagined. Throughout the Temple, the walls and doors were inlaid with solid gold. Jewels were inlaid into the walls to add to the beauty. However, in the intense heat of the fire, most of the gold had melted and flowed down between the stones of the Temple floor.

Roman excavators were called to the scene and began immediate excavation of the foundation to retrieve the gold. Soon, it was determined that it would be necessary for every foundation stone to be completely removed from the site. Thus, Christ's prophecy was fulfilled as "Not one stone here will be left on another; ... "[235]

Flavius Josephus, a first-hand witness to these events, recorded that some of the stones were ninety feet long, ten and a half feet high and thirteen feet wide. That's the size of a singlewide house trailer! Furthermore, he recorded that when all the foundation stones were removed from the site, a plow was used to run over the entire site where the Temple once stood, fulfilling the prophecy recorded some seven hundred years prior: "Zion shall be plowed as a field; Jerusalem shall become a heap of ruins."[236]

However, a number of outer wall stones were left unmoved and remain still today. The site is commonly known as the Jewish Wailing Wall. Apparently, Jesus was not speaking like an accountant, engineer, or physicist when he said "Not a stone upon a stone," but was using the ordinary colloquial language of the day for total destruction.

---

234. Ezekiel 16:41
235. Mark 13:2 NIV
236. Micah 3:12 RSV

The Jewish Historian and the Great Tribulation

It's all in who you know. A senior senator in Emperor Nero's court, Vespasian, captured the Jewish general Josephus, who was in charge of the Jewish defense of Galilee against the Romans. Josephus predicted that Vespasian would become emperor. When Vespasian became emperor, the Romans freed Josephus. Soon Josephus became friends with Vespasian's son, Titus, who would later lead the assault on Jerusalem.

Acting as a modern day Henry Kissinger, Josephus made several unsuccessful attempts to persuade Jerusalem to surrender before it was finally destroyed. Josephus went on to chronicle the events of the Roman-Jewish War in Aramaic, then in Greek. The Jewish War by Josephus is the most detailed historical account of the Roman-Jewish War that survives.

Josephus was a Jew, not a Christian. However, his immaculate and secular chronicles of the war appear to provide a first-hand account of the fulfillment of biblical prophecy. The following is an abbreviated outline of how the Great Tribulation of which Christ spoke took place in 70 A.D. The writings of Josephus will be referred to several times in the following pages as we take a brief look at the war timeline and a few details regarding some of the prophecy and horror that took place within the city.

Timeline of the Seven-Year Roman-Jewish War of A.D. 66–73

MAY 66 A.D. Jerusalem erupts in revolt against Rome. Civil war rages within the city of Jerusalem and Christians flee.

The Roman procurator Florus demands seventeen talents from the Jewish Temple treasury and triggers an abrupt escalation in the already inflamed Jewish tax revolt. The Roman garrison in Jerusalem is overrun by Jewish rebels, who take control of the city and challenge Rome head-on. Unable to manage the crisis, Florus is joined by the governor of Roman Syria, Cestius Gallus, in an effort to subdue the rebellion. Gallus attacks Jerusalem but unexpectedly withdraws and loses almost an entire legion (about six thousand professional Roman soldiers). Gallus is removed from his post and Emperor Nero appoints Vespasian general to crush the rebellion.

66–69 A.D. Galilee	The legions progress under the leadership of Vespasian.
68–69 A.D. Rome, Italy	Nero commits suicide and military operations are temporarily suspended.
70 A.D. Jerusalem	Vespasian's son, Titus is assigned complete military command and Jerusalem is surrounded.
April 70 A.D. Jerusalem	The Roman army arrives to prepare the siege.
May 10, 70 A.D. Dawn	Roman assault begins at the third wall of Jerusalem.

In the early morning siege, the Roman ballistas hurled one hundred-pound stones over the walls and into the city. This "stoning" is considered a fulfillment of Biblical prophecy.[237] Josephus records it this way:

> Admirable as were the engines constructed by all the legions, those of the tenth were of peculiar excellence. Their scorpions were of greater power and their stone-projectors larger, and with these they not only kept in check the sallying parties, but those also on the ramparts. The stones that were thrown were of the weight of a talent, and had a range of two furlongs and more. The shock, not only to such as first met it, but even to those beyond them for a considerable distance, was irresistible. The Jews, however, at the first, could guard against the stone; for its approach was intimated, not only to the ear by its whiz, but also, being white, to the eye by its brightness. Accordingly they had watchmen posted on the towers, who gave warning when the engine was discharged and the stone projected, calling out in their native language, 'The

---

237. Ezekiel 23:37–49

stone is coming,' on which those towards whom it was directed would separate, and lie down before it reached them. Thus it happened that, owing to these precautions, the stone fell harmless. It then occurred to the Romans to blacken it; when, taking a more successful aim, as it was no longer equally discernible in its approach, they swept down many at a single discharge." (Josephus, Jewish Wars, Book 5, chapter 6, section 3).

JUNE 2, 70 A.D. Might and Madness—Romans parade in full dress while famine grips city.

For four days, the Romans paraded in full dress uniform as Titus ceremoniously doled out the pay of every legionary. The Jews crowded the walls and windows of the city to watch the process. Again, Josephus enters Jerusalem in a futile attempt to negotiate surrender.

Inside the city, chaos and mayhem were the order of the day. The starving roved the city, violently taking food from women, children, and the aged, and killing those who resisted. Josephus stated that "children pulled the very morsels that their fathers were eating out of their very mouths, and what was still more to be pitied, so did the mothers do as to their infants." Josephus continues:

There was a certain woman who dwelt beyond Jordan, her name was Mary; her father was Eleazar, of the village Bethezob, which signifies the house of Hyssop. She was eminent for her family and her wealth, and had fled away to Jerusalem with the rest of the multitude, and was with them besieged therein at this time. The other effects of this woman had been already seized upon, such I mean as she had brought with her out of Perea, and removed to the city. What she had treasured up besides, as also what food she had contrived to save, had been also carried off by the rapacious guards, who came every day running into her house for that purpose. This put the poor woman into a very great passion, and by the frequent reproaches and imprecations she cast at these rapacious villains, she had provoked them to anger against her; but none of them, either out of the indignation she had raised against herself, or out of commiseration of her case, would take away her life; and if she found any food, she perceived her labors were for others, and not for herself; and it was now become impossible for her any way to find any more food, while the famine pierced through her very bowels and marrow, when also her passion was fired to a degree beyond the famine itself; nor did she consult with any thing but with her passion and the necessity she was in. She then attempted a most unnatural thing; and snatching up her son, who was a child sucking at her breast, she said, "O thou miserable infant! For whom shall I preserve thee in this war, this famine, and this sedition? As to the war with the Romans, if they preserve our lives, we must be slaves. This famine also will destroy us, even before that slavery comes upon us. Yet are these seditious rogues more terrible than both the other. Come on; be thou my food, and be thou a fury to these seditious varlets, and a by-word to the world, which is all that is now wanting to complete the calamities of us Jews." As soon as she had said this, she slew her son, and then roasted him, and ate the one half of him, and kept the other half by her concealed. Upon this the seditious came in presently, and smelling the horrid scent of this food, they threatened her that they would cut her throat immediately if she did not show them what food she had gotten ready. She replied that she had saved a very fine portion of it for them, and withal uncovered what was left of her son. Hereupon they were seized with a horror and amazement of mind, and stood astonished at the sight, when she said to them, "This is mine own son, and what hath been done was mine own doing! Come, eat of this food; for I have eaten of it myself! Do not you pretend to be either more tender than a woman, or more compassionate than a mother; but if you be so scrupulous, and do abominate this my sacrifice, as I have eaten the one half, let the rest be reserved for me also." After which those men went out trembling, being never so much affrighted at any thing as they were at this, and with some difficulty they left the rest of that meat to the mother. Upon which the whole city was full of this horrid action immediately; and while everybody laid this miserable case before their own eyes, they trembled, as if this unheard of action had been done by themselves. So those that were thus distressed by the famine were very desirous to die, and those already dead were esteemed happy, because they had not lived long enough either to hear or to see such miseries. (Josephus, Jewish Wars, Book 5, Chapter 3, Section 4).

JUNE 70 A.D. As prophesied by Christ[238] a wall is built around the city to quicken famine.

In a dedicated effort to seal in the defenders of the city and accelerate the famine, Titus ordered the erection of a wall, which would encircle the entire city, sealing the fate of Jerusalem. Many believe this action by Rome was a fulfillment of the prophecy of Christ: "For days will come upon you when your enemies will build an embankment around you, surround you and close you in on every side."[239] The circumvallation at Jerusalem was five miles of trench and wall with more than a dozen forts built along its length.

Jewish citizens captured outside the walls of the city during escape attempts were crucified. Upwards of 500 people a day were crucified until there was neither wood for crosses nor land to accommodate the victims. Josephus records, "So the soldiers, out of the wrath and hatred they bore the Jews, nailed those they caught, one after one way, and another after another, to the crosses, by way of jest, when their multitude was so great, that room was wanting for the crosses, and crosses wanting for the bodies."[240]

Many Jewish citizens swallowed gold coins before attempting their escape from the city. However, according to Josephus, this idea resulted in an unprecedented inhumane "butcher" of scores of thousands. Here's how he recorded the event:

> Hereupon some of the deserters, having no other way, leaped down from the wall immediately, while others of them went out of the city with stones, as if they would fight them; but thereupon they fled away to the Romans. But here a worse fate accompanied these than what they had found within the city; and they met with a quicker dispatch from the too great abundance they had among the Romans, than they could have done from the famine among the Jews; for when they came first to the Romans, they were puffed up by the famine, and swelled like men in a dropsy; after which they all on the sudden overfilled those bodies that were before empty, and so burst asunder, excepting such only as were skillful enough to restrain their appetites, and by degrees took in their food into

---

238. Luke 19:41–44
239. Luke 19:43 NKJV
240. Josephus, Jewish Wars, Book 5, chapter 11, Section 1

bodies unaccustomed thereto. Yet did another plague seize upon those that were thus preserved; for there was found among the Syrian deserters a certain person who was caught gathering pieces of gold out of the excrements of the Jews' bellies; for the deserters used to swallow such pieces of gold, as we told you before, when they came out, and for these did the seditious search them all; for there was a great quantity of gold in the city, insomuch that as much was now sold [in the Roman camp] for twelve Attic [drams], as was sold before for twenty-five. But when this contrivance was discovered in one instance, the fame of it filled their several camps, that the deserters came to them full of gold. So the multitude of the Arabians, with the Syrians, cut up those that came as supplicants, and searched their bellies. Nor does it seem to me that any misery befell the Jews that was more terrible than this, since in one night's time about two thousand of these deserters were thus dissected (Josephus, Jewish Wars, Book 5, chapter 13, section 4).

Ezekiel spoke of the tribulation this way:

"...Their silver and gold will not be able to save them in the day of the Lord's wrath. They will not satisfy their hunger or fill their stomachs with it, for it has made them stumble into sin. They were proud of their beautiful jewelry and used it to make their detestable idols and vile images. Therefore I will turn these into an unclean thing for them. I will hand it all over as plunder to foreigners and as loot to the wicked of the earth, and they will defile it. I will turn my face away from them, and they will desecrate my treasured place; robbers will enter it and desecrate it."[241]

APRIL 15, 73 A.D. Fall of Masada: Last of Jewish rebels fall.

Representing the final official act of the Roman-Jewish war, the last of the Jewish rebels fall to the Romans when the mountain fortress of Masada is taken after a lengthy siege.

---

241. Ezekiel 7:19–22 NIV

J. E. Lendon, associate professor of history at the University of Virginia, says that the Roman Siege of Jerusalem was "probably the greatest single slaughter in ancient history."[242] By the end of 73 A.D., it was estimated that 1.1 million Jews were slaughtered and ninety-seven thousand were taken captive.

Let's move on and talk about the needs and concerns of divorced people today. Approximately fifty percent of first marriages, sixty percent of second, and seventy percent of third marriages end in divorce. If you're in one of those groups, God's grace can cover you.

The War of Divorce in Our World

If you've been through a divorce, you would probably agree that there's no such thing as a "good" divorce. Divorce often tempts us to say things and do things that we may have previously thought unacceptable. It is often a cold and heartless battle for territory and possessions. It can be a brutal verbal war, whether insidious or outspoken, and is often a tragedy for all of those involved.

If you have a fantastic marriage, be compassionate toward those who don't. If there is someone in your circle of friends who has been divorced, look for ways to be a good friend. Never underestimate the pain of a broken marriage.

When you marry, you make a covenant before God. God values promises. He is a covenant-making God and he knows that broken covenants create broken people. If I tell you I'm going to do something and I don't do it, something inside you hurts. It's called heartbreak. If I am slow to keep a promise to my daughters, they will look at me and say, "But Daddy, you promised." Even though people tend to remember what you do, instead of what you say, the spoken word is one of the most powerful tools you have.

---

242. Lendon, J.E., Soldiers and Ghosts: A History of Battle in Classical Antiquity, New Haven, CT, Yale University Press, 2005

God's laws exist, not to restrict us as some may suppose, but for our protection and true happiness. Take a moment and imagine that a massive power outage occurred in your city and all of the traffic signals quit working for twenty-four hours.

There would be traffic jams for miles in all directions. Road rage and violence would be the scene at hundreds of accidents. Emergency medical vehicles would be stuck in traffic and delayed indefinitely as injured drivers suffered unnecessarily. Many, who would otherwise have been saved, would die.

Police would be almost completely helpless to control the looting that would quickly spread throughout the area. Calls for help would overwhelm 911 call centers and most people would not receive help for hours, perhaps days. Chaos and mayhem of unprecedented proportions would be wide spread. All of this because of a twenty-four-hour period without traffic signals.

It's safe to say that traffic signals don't restrict our driving pleasure, traffic signals create freedom and driving pleasure.

Like traffic signals, the things we often think restrict us actually provide the freedom, peace and happiness. This is why God gave us his word. Not to restrict us and cause us misery, but to provide the greatest freedom, peace and happiness available.

And in case you didn't know, obeying God also gives you ground for arguing a case with God. If you are paying your tithes from a heart of joy and obeying the word, when calamity strikes, you have a right to go to God in prayer, ask for what you want and expect an answer. That is the rule, not the exception. And when God answers your prayer, you shouldn't say, "Isn't that amazing!" Rather, we should be thinking "Okay, what else do I need?" By the way, it's interesting to note that the act of paying our tithes is a rare place in the scriptures: a place where God challenges us to challenge him. Another is Isaiah 7:11 where God said, "Ask the Lord your God for a sign, whether in the deepest depths or in the highest heights." In times of decision we should ask God for a sign!

Just like trying to live in a city without traffic signals, decisions to "go our own way" have consequences. For those who choose to go their own way, God will cause them to be delusional and full of fear.[243] God doesn't want us to live in sin. And he will always forgive us. God knows the consequences of sin will hurt us and fill our lives with unnecessary pain. He doesn't want us to hurt. Thus, the "traffic signals" of our life come in the form of God's commands and the teachings of Christ found in the Bible. If you want peace and stability in your life, start living your life according to the word of God, hit your knees regularly and ask for peace and stability. He's promised to answer you.

Are you separated from your spouse? If so, God wants you to make every effort to reconcile your relationship with your spouse. In some circumstances, this may not be an option, or it may not be the will of God.[244] However, the God who created this universe can recreate your marriage and your life. He's just waiting for you to open the door. He does the impossible first.

If you are divorced, repent, accept God's grace, and move forward. Divorce is not an unforgivable sin. Purpose in your heart to live a life that's pleasing to God from this point on. Perhaps the pain you've experienced has equipped you to minister unto others.

Divorce is often painful for the husband and wife, the children, grandparents and siblings. Divorce separates friends too. It often causes hate between the parties. Why must we hate? Hate is never a good idea. It causes people to make bad decisions. Divorce is a fact of life. How we handle it and how we treat the other party does matter.

It doesn't get any tougher than having somebody in your organization defect to the enemy, take a bribe, and give up your location. This is what Judas did to Christ. But Christ didn't hate him for it.

When the authorities came to arrest Christ, the other eleven followers quickly betrayed him. Even after being subjected to an illegal midnight session of court, falsely accused, beaten to near death, and then

---

243. Isaiah 66:3,4
244. Deuteronomy 24:1–5

Chapter 4: God Divorced His Bride

publicly humiliated on a cruel Roman cross until he died, Christ didn't hate. "Father, forgive them..." were the first words out of his mouth when the cross was hoisted into the air.

If you've been mistreated, Christ knows your pain. In fact, nobody knows it better. He had the power to stop the injustice and punish those who had rejected him. You may have the desire and opportunity to lash out, hurt, or even emotionally crush your former spouse. But what possible good can come from it? It's easy to stick a bumper sticker on your car that says, "What Would Jesus Do?" It's another thing to act like Christ when the whole world is yelling, "Crucify him!"

Divorce in the 21st Century

God's marriage and divorce illustrate both God's wrath and his mercy. If someone were to consider using this as an example for his or her own divorce, there are little grounds for doing so.[245] Moreover, the grounds that Christ gives for divorce are far more complicated than a simple act of sexual unfaithfulness.

There is a difference between adultery and fornication and they are listed separately in scripture.[246] Adultery is a breach of the marriage union. Adultery is any sexual activity between a married man and a woman other than his wife, and sexual activity between a married woman and a man other than her husband.

Fornication is two persons, both unmarried, having intercourse with each other. There is no cheating on a spouse, so there is no adultery. Fornication extends from a single or even a few isolated acts of immoral sex to every kind of illegal sexual intercourse in a list of sins,[247] including blatant, wanton sexual whoredom-casting all restraint aside, selling the body into a life of sexual impurity without remorse, guilt, or intention of repentance. Early descriptions of apostasy from God and

---

245. Malachi 2:14–16; I Corinthians 7:10–13
246. Matthew 15:19; Mark 7:21
247. Romans 1:29

idolatry are referred to as fornication.[248] The first three chapters of Hosea provide an illustration of how the nation of Israel had become guilty of fornication by going after other gods.

Some believe that Christ's description of lustful fantasizing of sex with someone other than your spouse[249] is a form of adultery. This may be the case. If so, it would include the viewing of pornography and would be different from simply being tempted. However, I believe that Christ was talking about "the heart" and what it meant to ancient Hebrews, Greeks, and Romans (i.e. the seat of the will, of our decisions). In this worldview, if we decide to commit adultery with a certain person, but never get the chance, God judges the heart (that is, the intention) and won't find the person innocent just because they didn't get their way.

Wishing for it, wanting it, feeling intoxicated about it while never intending to give into these feelings is normal and is not a sin. This is temptation. However, if you find a person extremely unattractive and wouldn't have sex with them if they were the last person in the world, there is no virtue in the fact that you don't have sex with them. You have a virtue only when you resist a temptation to sin. This challenge requires discipline and a desire for moral excellence.

Many have borne the burden of living with an unfaithful spouse. Many have gone on to file for divorce based upon those grounds. However, a closer look at the Scripture most commonly used by Christians who are seeking a divorce says, "And I say to you, whoever divorces his wife, except for sexual immorality, and marries another, commits adultery; and whoever marries her who is divorced commits adultery."[250]

Notice that Christ refers to fornication and then to adultery. They are two distinctively different sins. It could be easy to misinterpret this passage. Notice, Christ doesn't say, "If sexual immorality is committed, it is okay in the sight of God to divorce your spouse." Christ is addressing the issue of adultery, divorce, and remarriage. He is not giving his permission for divorce. He answered this issue earlier in verse 6, "Therefore what God has joined together, let man not separate."

---

248. Jeremiah 2
249. Matthew 5:27–28
250. Matthew 19:9 KJV

What is clear is that when a divorce is initiated because of fornication and the innocent party remarries another, the innocent party has not committed adultery in the sight of God. However, has the person who got the divorce done what is pleasing in the eyes of God? The scriptures give us direction in these kinds of matters. The apostle Paul wrote, "Live as children of light . . . and find out what pleases the Lord."[251]

Ask yourself this question: is lying a sin? The scriptures affirm that it is. However, it's safe to say that nobody can say they've never told a lie. But since we've all told a lie, does it mean that we should throw out the standard? Of course not. As Christians, we should repent of our lying, believe that God has forgiven us and stop lying.

Is lying forgiveable? Of course. The scriptures say, "If we confess our sins, He is faithful and just to forgive us our sins, ..."[252] The same applies to both divorce and remarriage. Both violate the divine principle of permanent union and faithfulness in marriage.

Christ warned that remarriage after divorce amounts to adultery, a sin which is explicitly forbidden by God's seventh Commandment. But, "The Lord is merciful and gracious, slow to anger, and plenteous in mercy . . . For He knoweth our frame; He remembereth that we are dust."[253] Therefore it is worth repeating, "If we confess our sins, He is faithful and just to forgive us our sins." This promise is specifically for Christians, and includes even the sin of adultery, if there is genuine repentance. The Lord made this very clear in His dealing with the woman who "... was taken in adultery, in the very act."[254] He reminded her religious accusers that they also were sinners and had no right to punish her.

Christ offered forgiveness to her without any conditions on her freedom, either to return to her husband, or to marry another if she were already divorced. He does, however, instruct her to, "... go, and sin no more."[255]

---

251. Ephesians 5:8–10 NIV
252. I John 1:9 KJV
253. Psalm 103:8, 14 KJV
254. John 8:4 KJV
255. John 8:11 KJV

On the other hand, Christ, who forgave the adulteress, never recommended a person divorce simply because the spouse fell into adultery one time. And what Christian person who loved their spouse would want divorce? For example, if you file for divorce because your spouse lost all of their money, this is a strong indication that you married for the wrong reason and didn't actually love your spouse.

The thing that sets Christianity apart from every other religion is forgiveness, mercy, and grace to transgressors. Millions of marriages have survived the wounds of adultery and the partners, scarred though they may be, go on to establish and maintain a solid marriage, home, and Christian testimony.

Adultery is a serious offense and its harm cannot be overemphasized. The book of Proverbs scorns adultery as a senseless act by which a man destroys his life.[256] It's that traffic signal thing again. Let the unfaithful beware: the New Testament specifically says that where there is no repentance, those who practice adultery will be excluded from eternity with God.[257] It is the exact opposite of loving one's neighbor as oneself[258] and falls under the direct judgment of God.[259]

A Godly Divorce: It's in the Bible

Some unsanctified marriages may have a partner who becomes a homosexual. Some husbands rape their wives. Some marriage partners are physically abusive to their spouse or conduct themselves as pagans, committing all kinds of fornication without repenting. This may include having sex with animals and sexual pleasures with their children or someone else's children.

If you have been taught that once you are married, you can never get a divorce because God hates divorce,[260] there is hope. This book is not intended as an endorsement for divorce, which should be approached

---

256. Proverbs 6:23–35
257. 1 Corinthians 6:9
258. Romans 13:9
259. Hebrews 13:4
260. Malachi 2:16

with the respect and fear that it deserves. However, there are unmistakable and important examples of Godly divorce recorded in the Bible. Let's take a look at one in particular.

The book of Ezra presents us with a scene where a large group of the priests' sons left town for a long weekend. Allow me to paint the scene for you this way: The guys jumped on a plane in Miami and flew to the Bahamas! While they were there they met some wild, Bahamian "bombshells!" They all fell in love and got married while on the island. On the next Monday afternoon, daunting straw hats and bright, colorful clothing the newlywed couples arrive at Miami International Airport. They locate their cars and head to a local restaurant where all of the parents are waiting to greet them. The parents are unaware that the boys have married and are about to get the shock of their life. The newlyweds are anxious to share their exciting news with the parents who are patiently waiting. Upon arriving at the restaurant the sons quickly realize that the parents are not happy. In fact, they're quite irate. One of the dads is a divorce attorney. He quiets the group and makes an announcement, "You all have lost your minds. These girls practice voodoo. You are all going to get divorced and God's going to bless it. Line up."

The priests' sons had married pagan wives and later came to Ezra, the priest, in repentance: "We have trespassed against our God, and have taken pagan wives from the peoples of the land; yet now there is hope in Israel in spite of this. Now therefore, let us make a covenant with our God to put away all these wives and those who have been born to them, according to the advice of my master and of those who trembled at the commandment of our God; and let it be done according to the law. Arise, for this matter is your responsibility. We also are with you. Be of good courage, and do it."[261] Ezra continues, "Now therefore, make confession unto the Lord God of your fathers, and do his pleasure: and separate [divorce] yourselves from the people of the land, and from the strange wives."[262]

---

261. Ezra 10:2–4 NKJV
262. Ezra 10:11 KJV

First, let's define "pagan." Here's the definition given by *The American Heritage Dictionary*: "n. 1. A person who is not a Christian, Muslim, or Jew; heathen. 2. One who has no religion. adj. 2. Not religious; heathen."

If you are considering a divorce, search the Scriptures for yourself, spend time in prayer, and seek advice and counsel from a committed Christian who is professionally trained to counsel on these matters. If you are married to a pagan, there's hope. It is apparent that God is directly opposed to a marriage between a believer and a pagan. The only other ground given in the scripture for divorce is desertion.[263]

My advice? Proceed with caution.

---

263. I Corinthians 7:15

Chapter

5 Forgive Everybody Everything

As Christians, there is much to be done to change the world for Christ. However, let's begin by cleaning up our own bedroom. We need to consider the motives of our hearts (the source of our words) and the tone in which we speak and are heard. What about our actions and our body language? They represent more than eighty percent of our personal communication to other people.

In 2005, it was my "year" (as a divorced parent) to be with my children during the Thanksgiving holiday. However, my former wife asked that I bring them over for dinner on the Saturday evening following Thanksgiving. She continued by explaining that some of our old friends would be there and that it could be a great party. The idea of me, her, and the children sitting around the table, sharing a holiday meal and celebrating Thanksgiving together with some old friends sounded like a good idea and I readily agreed.

At some point after our telephone conversation, she made arrangements for our long-time Christian friends to attend the dinner. However, she didn't mention to our friends that I would be there. But then, why would she need too, right?

My girls and I arrived early to help with the table and meal preparations. All was well until our friends arrived.

Once inside the home, the husband became angry and was filled with indignation because I was at the party and soon left the celebration in protest. To say the least, his words and deeds were discourteous and unnecessary. His actions and words conveyed the feelings that he was too good to be in the presence of a "sinner" like me. However, could it be that he was misinformed about the divorce and the details of the failed relationship between my former wife and I?

Now look at this man, this spiritual baby, retreating to his automobile, sulking in his self-righteousness. Is this what Christ would do? Are these actions those of a New Testament Christian? His disturbing behavior and boycott cast an icy tone over the entire holiday celebration, ruining the evening for all of the guests.

The older brother of the prodigal son demonstrates a classic case of an ill-tempered attitude. When his wayward brother repented and returned home the young man's father decided to have a party to celebrate the son's safe return. He killed the "fatted calf," called friends and family and proceeded to celebrate. The older brother became jealous of the attention the prodigal son was receiving. The older brother's self-righteousness bubbled to the top of his otherwise noble character. Full of envy and jealousy, he protested by leaving the party, chilling the festivities for some, if not all of the family and guests inside.

One Sunday morning in 2004, I attended a church I'd regularly attended some fifteen years earlier. As I slipped in the back door and chose a seat in the back row, I glanced to my left where a woman sat at the opposite end. Simultaneously, she turned and looked at me. Here was another old "friend" from church whom I hadn't seen in a dozen years or more.

Apparently, she too had heard some of the gossip regarding my failed marriage. When we made eye contact, her mouth dropped open. Glaring, she tilted her head slightly, squinted her eyes, pursed her lips, and with a pious look of indignation quickly gathered all of her things and moved to another area of the church.

Chapter 5: Forgive Everybody Everything

Through the years I've heard divorced people say they feel like an "outcast," yet I had no clue what they were talking about. Striking deep into the emotions, this incident drove the message home. And the irony of the story: This woman was once divorced and her current husband was a divorced man when she married him.

Nothing has done more to harm the cause of Christ than ill-tempered Christians. Neither stealing, lust for material wealth, drunkenness, fornication, nor adultery outweighs the sins represented in a single episode of ill temper. Why? Because words have the power of life and death. Ill-tempered words and deeds flow from the heart of a person and can be incredibly damaging. None of us are righteous. The heart of man is deceitful and desperately wicked.[264]

We all know people who would seem to be entirely perfect except for their easily offended, easily angered disposition. Ill temper: the principal vice of many who profess to be Christians.

The two unnamed people mentioned above are considered "pillars" in the churches where they attend. And I'm embarrassed to say that I've been guilty of the same kind of conduct. How many people reject the good news of the love of Christ because of the unkindness and self-righteous attitudes of people who claim to be Christians?

When it comes to breaking the spirit of a child, destroying relationships, fanning the flames of divorce, discouraging the hearts of men and women, planting the seeds of bitterness or starting wars, ill temper stands on its own. What are some of the symptoms? A lack of love for sinners, self-righteousness, jealousy of sinners, resentfulness, anger, cruelty, selfishness, greed, pride, bitterness, gossiping, murmuring, impatience, lack of courtesy, lack of kindness, lack of forgiveness, and lack of self control.

These are attitudinal sins. Although trustworthy and diligent, the older brother's sin was the greater sin of the two brothers.

Attempting to deal with the symptoms of ill temper is futile. We must go to the source, "For out of the overflow of the heart the mouth speaks.[265]

---

264. Romans 3:10; Jeremiah 17:9
265. Matthew 12:34 NIV

The symptoms of ill temper can be likened to the bubbles rising up from the carcass of a dead animal lying at the bottom of a beautiful, tree-lined lake. Everything looks good from a distance, but the water is deadly. To make the water suitable for any good purpose, the carcass must first be removed.

Located in the heart of Glenwood Springs, Colorado, is a four hundred-foot long swimming pool. It is one of the most popular tourist destinations within the city. What's truly unique about this pool is the water. The Yampah Hot Springs feeds the pool with a constant stream of steamy hot mineral-rich water that flows straight through the pool and then exits into the river beyond.

Each day three and a half million gallons of hot spring water flow through the pool. This constant flow of pure spring water keeps the pool water exceptionally clean even though there may be several hundred people relaxing in the pool at any given time.

Similarly, ill temper is not a problem when Christ flows into our lives. Daily reading of his word and time in prayer, a desire for the spirit of Christ in our life, and willingness to practice loving others like Christ did, and you are flowing. The love that comes from the Spirit of Christ inside us is the only source powerful enough to affect a positive change of heart, mind, soul, and body.

Only the Spirit of Christ can renew the mind of a person and repair and replace what is wrong within the soul. The apostle Paul declared the priority that love is the principal asset of life.

> If I speak with human eloquence and angelic ecstasy but don't love, I'm nothing but the creaking of a rusty gate. If I speak God's Word with power, revealing all his mysteries and making everything plain as day, and if I have faith that says to a mountain, "Jump," and it jumps, but I don't love, I'm nothing. If I give everything I own to the poor and even go to the stake to be burned as a martyr, but I don't love, I've gotten nowhere. So, no matter what I say, what I believe, and what I do, I'm bankrupt without love.[266]

---

266. I Corinthians 13:1–3 The Message

A tree can be identified quickly by its fruit. The people who live with you and come in contact with you on a daily basis will identify you as a Christian by the fruit you bear. Love, joy, peace, patience, kindness, goodness, faithfulness, gentleness, and self-control are the fruits of a Christian. They are essential elements, not optional equipment.

Spiritual gifts, talent, education, and obedience are not fruits. The apostle Paul stressed that your strict adherence to the law is not fruit. "Love God and neighbor" fulfilled and replaced[267] hundreds of regulations in the Pentateuch. Yes, I said "replaced." If you love your neighbor, you won't murder him, steal from him, lie to him, and so on. This is what Christ meant when he said, "A new command I give you: Love one another. As I have loved you, so you must love one another."[268]

Only a life that exemplifies the kindness of the Lord draws people to Christ. I've always believed that people don't care how much you know, until they know how much you care. So simple, yet so true.

In the spiritual world, our disposition identifies what spirit we have. A simple way to identify the fruits of the Holy Spirit in our life can be measured by our kindness and consideration for those who cannot do anything for us in return. Christ said, "... [W]hatever you did for one of the least of these brothers of mine, you did for me."[269] The question is; are the people we meet—whether a server at a restaurant, a lawn maintenance worker, or a telephone customer service agent who struggles with English—encouraged by the encounter, or are they happy to see us go?

Christ wrapped up his teaching on love as the most important thing in the world when he said, "But if anyone causes one of these little ones who believe in me to sin, it would be better for him to have a large millstone hung around his neck and to be drowned in the depths of the sea."[270] In other words, Christ says that it would be better for you to die an untimely death than to allow your words and actions to become the fruits of an ill-tempered disposition. Christ summed up the entire Bible when he said love God and your neighbor as yourself.[271]

---

267. John 13:34,35; 15:12–14
268. John 13:34 NIV
269. Matthew 25:40 NIV
270. Matthew 18:6 NIV

Christ's love is shared with others through people. To love others in the way that Christ loved others requires a conscious effort. Sincere love for our neighbors will only overtake us when we deliberately and relentlessly dedicate our life to acquiring the fruits of the Holy Spirit. Christ has been generous to us and we must be generous to others. "From everyone who has been given much, much will be demanded."[272]

Loving others as Christ loves them is defined by our actions. Our actions display whether our fruits are from the spirit of Christ or another spirit. Treating others as Christ treated people is the most important thing we can do. Through your everyday actions, share the kindness of Christ with those inside and outside of your home. The love of Christ is a verb…use words when necessary!

271. Matthew 22:36–40
272. Luke 12:48NIV

Notes From the Author

I tend to take the words and stories in the Bible literally, unless a symbolic message is intended. Faith that Christ is the Son of God is not complex. Once accepted, simply draw your attention to the bottom line: "... [H]ere is the conclusion of the matter: Fear God and keep his commandments, for this is the whole duty of man."[273]

Prayer is vital to spiritual success. Prayer is the only thing the disciples asked Jesus to teach them because they could see that's where Jesus drew his strength and direction. So pray already! Ask God to help you make wise decisions.

Can you be a different person today than you were yesterday? God says, "I will give you a new heart and put a new spirit in you; I will remove from you your heart of stone and give you a heart of flesh. And I will put my spirit in you and move you to follow my decrees and be careful to keep my laws."[274] God said he will "move you" (cause you) to follow his decrees..." God can give you a new heart and cause you to want to do his will! This type of success comes from reading and knowing the word and from spending time in prayer.

If you purchase an airline ticket and travel to Chennai, India, you can make an interesting observation as the airplane lands and taxis to the

---

273. Ecclesiastes 12:13, 14 NIV
274. Ezekiel 36:26, 27 NIV

end of the runway. Looking out the window on one side of the aircraft, you will notice a small, barren hill with a small church on top. The hill is called St. Thomas' Mount. 160 steps lead from the bottom to the top of the hill.

Few, if any, passengers on board would notice the small hill and it's safe to say that even fewer would recognize it as the traditionally recognized place of martyrdom for Saint Thomas. Doubting Thomas, that is. The traditional burial place of the apostle is located only a few minutes away in an area called Mylapore. The apostle arrived in India in A.D. 52 and was martyred around A.D. 75. Thomas brought the gospel to India and was buried in Mylapore after his death.

In Christian missionary work, some people are called by Christ to go; and some just...go. Thomas was called. Consequently, Thomas travelled further than any other apostle to spread the gospel. Considered by many as perhaps the greatest skeptic in all of the New Testament, Thomas launched countless Christian churches across India and may have traveled as far as China. The question is; what changed this pessimist into such a strong believer?

As the rumor of the resurrection of Christ circulated all across town, Thomas struggled with doubt and unbelief. From what he's seen, Christ had died a brutal death on a rugged Roman cross.

On the second Sunday after the resurrection, Thomas walked up a dusty side street in Jerusalem. Tapping softy on the door of the small house, he slipped inside the dark room where all of the other disciples were hiding in fear behind locked doors. However, once inside, Thomas would soon "see the light."

Their secret meeting was soon interrupted as Christ suddenly appeared in the room. Terrified, Christ calms their fears and then does something interesting. He asks, "Do you have anything here to eat?" Christ was always talking about breaking bread together! I wonder if he was smiling when he asked?

Their champion was alive! Raised from the dead. The eleven watched in amazement as he stood in their circle, eating the flame-broiled fish.[275] Then he made a statement and they finally "got it:"

Everything I told you while I was with you comes to this: All the things written about me in the Law of Moses, in the Prophets, and in the Psalms have to be fulfilled.... ...you can see now how it is what is written: The Christ will suffer and rise from the dead on the third day, and repentance and forgiveness of sins will be preached in his name to all nations, beginning at Jerusalem. You are witnesses of these things. I am going to send you what my Father has promised; but stay in the city until you have been clothed with power from on high.[276]

One encounter with the resurrected Christ and Thomas the skeptic became Thomas the crusader, never again doubting or wondering "who" Christ was. Then Thomas made history: he became the first person in the New Testament to recognize the divinity of Christ and proclaim him as God![277]

Here's the question: if Christ hadn't risen from the dead, would a skeptic like Thomas have risked his life for the next forty-plus years spreading the Good News? Would he have labored to build countless numbers of churches across the East and then die a martyr's death? Not a "doubting" Thomas. It's safe to say that neither would a sophisticated doctor like Luke, or a brilliantly educated genius like Paul, a street-wise, rough-neck, fishermen like Peter, or a savvy accountant like Matthew. Only a person who'd seen the resurrected savior would preach to the death the good news of Christ.

The next time you have doubts about God, remember: you're in good company! Thomas went further than all the rest to spread the gospel. And you can make a difference too. Trust Christ to help you. "Doubt your doubts and believe your beliefs." Then get on with sharing the good news of Christ!

In Christ, there's hope for everyone who'll confess their sins and accept Christ as their savior. Sharing that message with others is up to you and I. When your life ends, what will you render unto the Lord for all of his many benefits toward you?[278]

Is he knocking on your heart's door now? What will your answer be?

---

275. Luke 24:42,43
276. Luke 24:44–53 The Message
277. John 20:28
278. Psalms 116:12

Jesus Drank, Judas Repented and God Divorced His Bride

Bibliography

The Holy Bible-KJV, King James Version (Michigan: Zondervan Publishing House, 1992).

The Holy Bible-NIV, New International Version (Michigan: Zondervan, 2004).

The Holy Bible, The Message Version (Michigan: Zondervan, 2004).

The Holy Bible, New Living Translation (Illinois: Tyndale House, 1996).

The Holy Bible-NKJV, New King James Version (Tennessee: Thomas Nelson, 1989).

The Holy Bible-RSV, Revised Standard Version (Michigan: Zondervan Publishing House, 1992).

The Holy Bible-NCV, New Century Version (Tennessee: Thomas Nelson, 1991).

The NKJV Greek-English Interlinear New Testament (Tennessee: Thomas Nelson, 1994).

The Septuagint, (London, England, Samuel Bagster & Sons, Ltd., 1851).

Henry, Matthew, Matthew Henry's Complete Commentary on the Whole Bible, Vol. I, II, III, IV, V, VI, (1706–1721).

Josephus, Flavius, The War of The Jews, http://www.gutenberg.org/etext/2850.

Lendon, J. E., Soldiers and Ghosts: A History of Battle in Classical Antiquity, (New Haven, CT, Yale University Press, 2005).

The American Heritage Dictionary, Houghton Mifflin Company, (Massachusetts, 1979).

Conard, Audrey. "The Fate of Judas: MT 27:3–10 (redactional analyses)." Toronto Journal of Theology. 7 (Fall 1991): 158–168.

About the Author

Steve Brown

Divorce was a life changing experience for me. I felt Christ still cared and had forgiven me, but it was obvious that many Christians looked at me contemptuously. Discouraged, I began searching the scriptures to learn what the Bible actually says about divorce. What I discovered is that God divorced his own bride (Isaiah 50:1) and that a divorce of hundreds of people pleased God (Ezra 10:11.) Every new discovery created a greater desire to learn more. The more I looked, the more I found.

For example, Matthew 27:3 states that Judas Iscariot repented, confessed his "sin" publicly and returned the money. I'd never heard anybody expound on these facts. While nobody can prove the final disposition of Judas, the scriptures provide compelling evidence that he found grace.

As I studied I found a few primary stories that, even though some may not be "life-changing" accounts, were quite provocative. For example, I had never been taught that Noah took fourteen reindeer on the ark (Genesis 7:2.) Then, when I discovered the true story of David and Goliath, I wanted my children to know about it. I wanted them to know why David ran from Goliath (I Samuel 17:24) and I wanted them to know why he went back and killed Goliath. This is a powerful, life-changing story and one that has gone virtually untold.

With heavy research and hundreds of footnotes, *Jesus Drank, Judas Repented and God Divorced His Bride* is a roller-coaster ride through Bible facts, history, and sensitive life subjects that have been ignored for centuries by mainstream Christians.

Other Happy About Books

Read this book if you want to laugh, cry, and be inspired.

Many of us wish that we could lead lives of service, and would prefer one day to leave the world a better place because we were in it while others are on a quest for personal redemption.

Paperback: $16.95
eBook: $14.95

Care: You Have the Power!

The vignettes in *Care: You Have the Power!* from a Hall of Fame football quarterback to company CEOs to participants in homeless shelters renew our faith and lead to action in utilizing care factors in our lives starting right now.

Paperback: $19.95
eBook: $14.95

Moving From Vision to Reality

This book combines Christian spirituality with leadership principles to allow you to fulfill your 'true' purpose in life.

Paperback $19.95
eBook $14.95

140 Perspectives on Being a Supportive Witness to the End of Life

In #DEATH tweet Book02, Timothy Tosta addresses the fearful and emotional issue of how we support a loved one at the end of her or his life journey. How do we face our own uncertainties?

Paperback: $19.95
eBook: $14.95

Purchase at http://happyabout.com or at other online and physical bookstores.

9 781600 052019